Law and Society

Michelle Cale

Printed cartoon submitted in the libel action brought by William Long, surgeon at St Bartholomew's Hospital against S W Fores, printer for publishing a print 'intended to ridicule this Deponent in the exercise and discharge of his professional and official duties.' The patient, Louis Barthelmicci, subsequently died of wounds inflicted by a poker. Enclosed with William Long's affidavit – King's Bench Division: Affidavits KB 1/30 (Easter Term 40 Geo III no 18).

Public Record Office Readers' Guide No 14

Law and Society

An Introduction to Sources for
Criminal and Legal History
from 1800

Michelle Cale

PRO Publications

The author would like to express her thanks to Jack Cantwell for all the hard work he contributed to this volume in bringing it to completion.

PRO Publications
Public Record Office
Ruskin Avenue
Kew
Surrey
TW9 4DU

20026005

Contents

Illustrations

Cover illustration (front) features a detail from a lithographed contract drawing for the New
    Courts of Justice in the Strand, 1871, showing the Carey Street elevation WORK
    30/1991, and (back) a section of Newgate prison gallows HO 144/18/46327

Using the Public Record Office

At the time of writing (1996) the records held by the Public Record Office (PRO) are divided between two sites, at Kew and Chancery Lane. The present whereabouts of the records described in this guide is set out at section 1.1.2. If you are in doubt about which site to visit, telephone beforehand. By the end of 1996 it is envisaged that the Chancery Lane building will close and all original records will be housed at Kew, but certain popular classes viewed on microfilm will be seen at a central London microfilm reading room.

Public Record Office, Ruskin Avenue, Kew, Surrey TW9 4DU.

Public Record Office, Chancery Lane, London WC2A 1LR.

The telephone number is the same for both sites: **0181-876-3444**.

The Office is open from 9.30 am to 5.00 pm Monday to Friday. The Census Rooms and the Microfilm Reading Room at Chancery Lane are also open from 9.30 am to 5.00 pm on Saturdays. You do not need to make an appointment. The office is closed on public holidays and for annual stocktaking (usually the first two weeks in October). The museum and shop are open from 9.30 am to 4.45 pm.

When you first visit the PRO, please bring with you formal documentary proof of identity bearing your name and signature. If you are not a British citizen you will need to bring your passport or national identity card. You will then be issued with a Reader's Ticket. Without a valid ticket you cannot be admitted to the reading rooms or order documents. You do not need one to visit the Census Rooms, Microfilm Reading Room or the Museum at Chancery Lane.

You may use only graphite pencils in the reading rooms. Pens of any kind are not allowed. You may use personal computers, typewriters and tape recorders in designated areas. A full list of Reading Room rules is available on request.

Each document has a unique three-part reference. The first part is the lettercode, for example CP for the Court of Common Pleas, E for the Exchequer, HO for Home Office and J for the Supreme Court of Judicature, according to the provenance of the documents, but with the growth of bureaucracy the letters given do not necessarily bear any resemblance to the body concerned, eg Council on Tribunals is BL. The second part is the class number, which represents the series within the lettercode; these often equate to types of documents, for example affidavits, depositions or indictments. The third part is the piece number, which represents the individual document.

To identify the lettercode and class, consult the published Current Guide, which is the primary guide to the holdings of the PRO. The Current Guide is in three parts. Part 1 describes the history and functions of government departments. Part 2 briefly describes each class with information such as the covering dates and number of pieces. Part 3 is the index to the other two parts. There is no general detailed index covering records in the PRO. Once possible classes have been identified, the next step is to consult the class lists which briefly describe each piece. These are available in the PRO reading or reference rooms. For a working example of how to find the reference for a particular piece from one of the more complicated class lists see Appendix I.

For some further advice on using the PRO see Section 1.1.4.

Chapter 1: INTRODUCTION

1.1 Scope

This guide is a survey of those records held by the Public Record Office (PRO) which would be useful for historical research into aspects of the law and crime. It does not pretend to be exhaustive. Its objectives are, firstly, to make the reader more aware of the existence of such records and, secondly, to help the reader better appreciate the possibilities which they offer in a number of subject areas. Essentially, this survey is an introductory reference work, intended to help you work out where to begin your investigations; however, this does not always mean that the PRO will or should necessarily be your first port of call.

While writing this guide, it became clear to me that a survey of this kind could not hope to do justice to commercial and property law. These are immense, complex subjects which richly deserve their own special publications. They have been, therefore, largely omitted from this book. Neither does it deal, except briefly (2.2.14), with Administrative tribunals, comparatively few of whose records have yet been transferred to the PRO. Readers interested in manorial courts, which dealt with minor disputes between tenants, copyhold inheritance and behaviour against the common good, will also be disappointed. Another PRO publication: Mary Ellis, *Using Manorial Records, PRO Readers' Guide No 6* (1994) explains where such records are to be found.

1.1.1 Definitions

This thing we refer to as 'the Law' can be divided up and described in many ways. **Public law**, for example, concerns the organization and functions of government agencies, such as central government departments and local councils, and their relationship with each other and the ordinary citizen. **Private law**, on the other hand, is concerned with the legal relationships of ordinary individuals, including matters such as divorce, the making of contracts, and transfer of property.

Criminal law is a form of public law which identifies undesirable conduct which will attract punishment by the state. The **civil law**

encompasses private law and also certain elements of public law, such as applications for judicial review of the decisions of government bodies.

The **common law** is based on customs and precedents created through judicial decisions and recorded in **case law** (for which see the Law Reports described at 1.3.4). It is distinct from **statutory law** which is, as the name suggests, law based on legislation passed by parliament which may also abolish or amend common law rules. To overcome the rigidities of the common law **equity** was developed (see 2.2.2), but subsequently developed rigidities of its own. Finally, **canon law** consists of the rules which are in force in ecclesiastical or church courts. The work of church courts today is principally concerned with the conduct of clergy; however, before 1857 canon law was of much broader significance as the church courts were responsible for dealing with wills, matrimonial causes and enforcing standards of morality.

In this guide, the phrase 'criminal justice system' is used to describe collectively the work of all the agencies concerned with crime detection, trial, sentencing and punishment.

1.1.2 Division of the Records in the PRO

At the time of writing, the records described in this survey are split between the PRO's two sites, at Ruskin Avenue in Kew and at Chancery Lane in central London, as follows:

Chancery Lane
B, C, CP, CRIM, DEL, DPP, HCA, KB, E, IND, J, LO, PALA, PC, PRIS, RG, TS

Kew
ADM, AIR, AO, ASSI, AST, BA, BC, BF, BL, BN, BS, BT, BV, ED, HLG, HO, LCO, MEPO, MH, MT, PCOM, PIN, PMG, PRO, T, WO, WORK, ZJ

All Chancery Lane classes of original records will be transferred to Kew in the course of 1996 at the end of which the Chancery Lane office is due to close. You are advised to telephone (0181-876-3444) in advance of your visit to determine availability.

1.1.3 The Availability of Public Records

The majority of records held by the PRO are subject to the 'thirty-year rule', i.e. they are closed to the public for thirty years after the last date on the file. Certain records are closed for longer periods, usually fifty, seventy-five or one hundred years. Some of the records described in this guide are subject to extended closure, generally because they contain sensitive personal information relating to individuals who are probably still living.

1.1.4 More Words of Advice on Using the PRO

- Information leaflets on particular topics are available on site. The following are a few words of advice based on experience, in no particular order.

- If you are using Kew local facilities are limited. Buy your newspaper, go to the bank and, unless you intend to eat in the restaurant on site, obtain your lunch near where you live. There is limited car parking on site for the public at Kew, but none at Chancery Lane.

- Arrive as early in the morning as you can, remembering that the office opens at 9.30 am, and try to order your first batch of documents almost at once. Later in the morning, the reading rooms can become rather crowded and the production of documents slows considerably under the weight of orders. This is particularly true during the summer months. It is intended to extend opening hours in 1997.

- At the beginning of your research, be prepared to spend a good half-day looking at lists of documents (commonly referred to as 'class lists') and other finding aids. Work out what you must see, what you want to see and what would be nice to see if you have time. When you are ordering, stick to your plan and you will save yourself time and frustration.

- You can order three documents (or 'pieces') at a time. When the first three arrive, order the next three. It is important to try to keep them flowing, so that you are never left without anything to do; but, equally, it is important that you do not order too much so that you feel compelled to rush. As with so much else in life, striking a balance comes with experience.

- As previously stated the use of ink and ballpoint pens in the reading rooms is prohibited. Take several pencils; and note that the propelling kind will save you constant trips to the sharpener. In addition, invest in a reasonably-sized magnifying glass which will be a great help in deciphering all those badly written, faded, fragile records.

- Finally, do not go to the PRO in your best clothes. Old documents can be very dirty indeed. The chances are that you will become rather grubby during the course of a day's research, so you should dress comfortably with this in mind.

1.2   Records outside the PRO

1.2.1 The National Register of Archives

The National Register of Archives (NRA) is an impressive computerized database containing details of the location of manuscripts useful for a study of British history. In general, it does not include information on the collections in the PRO. The NRA is made available at the Historical Manuscripts Commission's search room at Quality House, Quality Court, Chancery Lane, London WC2A 1HP. The Commission will answer limited and specific enquiries by post without charge. A range of free information sheets is available.

It is well worth using the NRA at the beginning of your research or if you cannot find the records of a particular organization or person. The NRA includes information about collections in a wide range of institutions, such as the libraries of cathedrals, universities and schools, as well as local authority record offices around the country and private individuals. The elusive papers may well turn up somewhere quite unexpected!

1.2.2 Local Record Offices

If you have never been to your local record office, find out where it is. You can find its address in *Record Repositories in Great Britain* (HMSO, 1994). Investigate the resources it has on offer. The majority of local record offices have extensive local history collections, both of original and secondary source material and normally hold **quarter sessions**, **county court** and **coroners' records**. For many researchers, almost everything they need to use will be there. A later visit to the PRO will be simply filling in gaps or enhancing the knowledge acquired locally.

Even if your interests lie outside the local area, the local record office will probably hold a range of biographical dictionaries, trade directories, catalogues and other reference works the use of which will help to shape your research in its early stages and possibly save you time when you visit the PRO.

1.3   Printed sources

There are a wide range of sources of information on legal and criminal history, quite aside from manuscript sources such as the papers in the care of the PRO. Indeed, in many instances, you will not be able to settle upon a suitable topic for research or make much sense of the records you see at the PRO until you have practically exhausted these alternatives.

Good public or university libraries should be able to provide access to at least some of the following.

1.3.1 Parliamentary Papers

For anyone interested in the nineteenth century, British parliamentary papers are an extraordinarily valuable printed source, and can be seen at Kew in microform. These copious papers cover a great multitude of subjects, from the efficacy of transportation to the diet of convicts and much else besides. You will find items such as annual judicial statistics; the reports and evidence of investigative Royal Commissions and Departmental Committees and specially prepared statistics and information eg *Report of the Royal Commission on Reformatory and*

Industrial Schools with Minutes of Evidence (Sessional Papers, House of Commons, C 3876, 1884, XLVI); *Rules for the Guidance of Officers, etc, of Broadmoor Criminal Lunatic Asylum* (Sessional Papers, House of Commons, 517, 1863, XLVIII, 329), *Return of Number of Corporal Punishments Inflicted in HM Prisons in 1881* (Sessional Papers, House of Commons, 230, 1882, LIV, 519); annual reports of government inspectors, for example of reformatories and convict prisons; and much more.

However, though well worth the effort, the uninitiated may not find it particularly easy to navigate their way around the numerous volumes of parliamentary papers and their indexes. If you have never used them before, ask a librarian or archivist to give you some guidance and you will save yourself time and frustration.

1.3.2 Statutes

Statutes rarely, in themselves, prove to be an appropriate starting point for research but they can be invaluable in clarifying the legal framework of institutions and social policies. Again, a good library should be able to provide printed sets of statutes and guidance on how to use them. Bill papers and associated files concerning Acts of Parliament from 1900 may be traced from the Legislation Index at Kew.

1.3.3 Newspapers

Local newspapers often carried descriptions of trials, sentencing and executions, generally written in a fairly sensational (and often amusing) style. While they are another splendid source of information, you would do well to remember not to believe everything you read!

The British Library has the most comprehensive collection of newspapers in the country at its Newspaper Library, Colindale Avenue, London NW9 5HE. Readers keen to use newspapers might find two introductory publications from the Federation of Family History Societies of particular help: *Local Newspapers 1750-1920: A Select Location List* by J S W Gibson; and *Family History from Newspapers* by Eve McLaughlin.

1.3.4 Law Reports

The daily decisions of courts in individual cases form the basis for the ever developing common law. Fortunately for the researcher investigating an aspect of the civil law (and, indeed, the lawyer), since 1865 the Incorporated Council of Law Reporting has been producing **Law Reports**, a series of reports on cases which are revised by the judges who heard them, prior to their publication. The less authoritative, but widely circulated, **All England Law Reports** have been produced on a weekly basis since 1936. Again, these publications should be available at a good public library. *The Times*, which can be seen at Kew in microform, and other newspapers also carry law reports.

Please note: Nothing in this guide should be taken to be an authoritative statement of British law as it presently stands.

Chapter 2: ADMINISTRATION OF THE LAW

2.1 The Personnel of the Legal System

2.1.1 The Lord Chancellor

The lord chancellor is Speaker of the House of Lords, the head of the judiciary, and the holder of a senior ministerial position in the government. He is chairman of the Judicial Committee of the Privy Council and has responsibility for recommending judicial appointments to the crown, overseeing the administration of the courts and legal aid, and reforming the civil law as necessary. A brief summary of the early history of this post is given in the section on the Court of Chancery (2.2.2). Since 1992 the lord chancellor has been assisted by a parliamentary secretary in the House of Commons.

Most of the lord chancellor's responsibilities are administered through the **Lord Chancellor's Department**. The records of this department in LCO classes touch on all aspects of the practical functioning of the court system and the policy considerations which have affected it. These records are described in detail in a valuable survey work by Patrick Polden, *Guide to the Records of the Lord Chancellor's Department* (HMSO, 1988), which concentrates particularly on the files in LCO 1 and LCO 2, but covers the whole range of the Department's responsibilities from about 1870 to 1951. References to LCO pieces will be found throughout later sections of this guide.

2.1.2 The Home Secretary

The responsibilities of the home secretary, a senior minister in the government, extend widely over the criminal justice system, including the creation of policy concerning prisons, probation, and policing. Until 1992 the home secretary was also responsible for the administration of magistrates' courts.

The personal papers of individual home secretaries are not to be found at the PRO. Many are deposited in national or local authority record offices.

For researchers interested in tracing these, a starting point is provided by the Historical Manuscripts Commission's publication *Papers of British Cabinet Ministers 1782-1900* (HMSO, London, 1982). Records of the home secretary's department, the **Home Office**, are kept at the PRO. References to these HO classes will be found throughout the remainder of this guide. Researchers using Home Office records for the first time may find Jill Pellew, *The Home Office 1848-1914* (Heinemann, 1982) useful preliminary reading. Before 1782, similar records created by the secretary of state will be found in the State Papers, Domestic, under the SP lettercode.

2.1.3 The Attorney-General

The attorney-general is a senior barrister who is usually a member of parliament. He is one of the two law officers who presently act for the crown, the other being the solicitor-general. The appointment is political, though the attorney-general is not a member of the Cabinet. The office's duties include representing the crown in certain international disputes, such as cases at the European Court of Human Rights, and advising the government generally on issues in English law.

The surviving records relating to the attorney-general's work are to be found not only among those of his own Law Officers' Departments in LO classes, but also among those of the Home Office, Treasury Solicitor and other departments. A small number of papers can be found in LCO 1 and LCO 2, while classes TS 16, LO 2 and a few others include some miscellaneous items. The main bulk of the papers dealing with the attorney-general's duties will be found among the Home Office records. HO 119 includes cases bearing his legal opinions. For example, in *Rex* v *Davies*, 1833 (HO 119/17), the attorney-general gave his opinion that a sentence of transportation passed erroneously upon a convicted person by a magistrate remained valid even though it was not laid down by the law. These papers throw light on a range of issues, including problems of evidence and sentencing, definition of offences and reliability of witnesses. Similar material can be found in HO 48/17. The cases noted in this volume are discussed and examined in great depth and though it has no index it is eminently browsable. Of particular interest are the cases involving accusations of high treason, such as the case brought against one Charles Smith for bearing arms in France against the English king in 1810. In this instance, the attorney-general's opinion was sought on whether there was sufficient evidence to prove that Smith was English for the case to proceed. He thought not, and advised that the case be dropped. Copies of Home Office letters to the attorney-general requesting advice or commenting on advice rendered, 1762 to 1871, can be seen in class HO 49. In general, law officers' opinions are to be found among the records of the department requesting the opinion, but there are a number on a variety of matters in TS 25.

Another aspect of the attorney-general's duties which is chronicled in Home Office series is his involvement in drawing up warrants for the creation of peerages and elevation to the peerage. For this, see in particular HO 116/4, letters dealing with creations and elevations between 1859 and 1888; and HO 143/1 which includes details of fees paid to the attorney-general on the creation of baronetcies between 1869 and 1875. Briefs in respect of peerage claims are in TS 16.

A little information on the daily work of the attorney-general can be gleaned from the letters in PRO 30/51 which were received by Hugh McCalmont Cairns, 1st Earl Cairns, who was attorney-general in 1866 before going on to be lord chancellor.

2.1.4 The Director of Public Prosecutions (DPP)

The office of director of public prosecutions was created by the Prosecution of Offences Act 1879. Before that date, no single authority had been responsible for giving advice on or taking forward public prosecutions. The Home Office had advised police forces and magistrates' clerks on possible prosecutions and had given directions to the Treasury Solicitor to institute proceedings in the most important cases, which generally encompassed politically motivated crimes. Following the creation of the DPP's office, there was a transitional period in which it shared responsibility with the Treasury Solicitor. For a short period after the turn of the century, the two offices were merged, but they were soon separated due to increasing pressure of work.

The DPP is supervized by and accountable to the attorney-general. He is head of the Crown Prosecution Service (CPS), which was established in 1985. No records relating to the CPS have yet been deposited at the PRO.

Many records of the DPP's office and functions are subject to an extended closure period of seventy-five years. They include registers of cases, 1884-1956 (DPP 3), and case papers, 1889-1983 (DPP 1 and DPP 2). Transcripts of proceedings in selected criminal trials, 1846-1958, are preserved in DPP 4. Class DPP 6, which includes papers on policy, procedure and instances of legal advice, is of more use to researchers seeking to trace the relationship between the DPP and other law officers and government departments in the twentieth century.

There are a small number of pieces in class LCO 1 relating to the work of the DPP, the most important of which is LCO 1/78 containing regulations for the work of the public prosecutor dated 1885-1886; and LCO 2 includes a memorandum of procedure in trials for high treason by the then DPP (LCO 2/3073).

Correspondence between the Treasury and DPP is preserved in T 15, and papers touching on the appointment of staff, their salaries and other related matters concerning the Public Prosecutions Department are available as T 221/326 and T 221/517.

2.1.5 The Treasury Solicitor

The treasury solicitor provides legal services for many government departments, including representing those departments in court proceedings to which they are a party and offering general advice on the interpretation of the law. For example, class TS 1 consists of the entry books for letters, 1859-1869, relating to prosecutions undertaken on behalf of the Royal Mint (for later prosecutions for the Royal Mint, see MINT 15). Class T 141 consists of three volumes of out-letters from the treasury solicitor's office, 1914-1921. Earlier correspondence dealing with fees, salaries and other payments can be found in T 15 and T 16. General series of papers are in TS 11 and TS 18, and there are a number of classes of files relating to particular departments of which TS 27, dealing with Treasury and Miscellaneous matters, is especially noteworthy.

The treasury solicitor's office was involved in the prosecution of those taking part in the Jacobite rebellion of 1745. Papers relating to this episode are preserved in TS 11 and TS 20, and records relating to the trials are in KB 8. Other papers in TS 11 and TS 24 relate to prosecutions for seditious acts, especially of those involved in the radical movements of the late-eighteenth and early-nineteenth centuries, and include copies of publications considered to be seditious. The TS 11 class also includes papers regarding the Chartist movement, riots and disturbances, and the inquiry into the conduct of Queen Caroline. Material relating to the prosecution of war crimes during the Second World War is in TS 26. Further papers relating to the treasury solicitor's role in the investigation of such crimes can be found in WO 310, WO 311 and WO 325.

Records of the treasury solicitor relating to the administration of *bona vacantia*, principally concerning the residuary estate of persons who have died intestate and without relatives, are mainly in TS 17.

2.1.6 Attorneys, Solicitors and Barristers

Attorneys had been part of the English legal system since the twelfth century, performing many of the functions we would now expect of a solicitor, particularly in the courts of the King's Bench and Common Pleas. They were first subjected to external regulation under the Attorneys' Act 1402 (4 Henry IV. c 18) which demanded that practising and prospective attorneys should be examined by judges to assess their honesty and grasp of the law and that the names of those approved to engage in the attorney's profession should have their names entered upon a roll.

Among the records of the Court of the King's Bench are KB 105 to KB 107, which consist of affidavits of the due execution of articles of clerkship. There are four sets of contemporary finding aids to these records which are at present part of class IND 1, some of which will be of particular interest to family historians seeking an ancestor in the legal profession: **registers** (IND 1/4568-4573 and IND 1/29722-29728), in which the affidavits are entered chronologically by date of filing, with a note of the names of the clerk and his attorney; **indexes** (IND 1/4577-4582 and IND 1/29734-29736), which are arranged alphabetically by the surname of the clerk and provide a cross-reference to the registers by giving the register entry number; **rolls of attorneys** (IND 1/4583-4592 and IND 1/29714-29717), arranged chronologically but with entries grouped by the first letter of the attorneys' names; and **attorneys' residence books** (IND 1/4593-4595), which give each attorney's name and address.

For similar records relating to the Court of the Common Pleas see: CP 8, Common Pleas Attorneys' Admission Rolls 1838-1860; CP 10, Common Pleas Attorneys' Oath Rolls, 1789-1847; CP 11, Common Pleas Rolls of Attorneys 1730-1750; and CP 5, Common Pleas Articles of Clerkship,

1730-1838, with indexes in IND 1/4596-4608 and IND 1/29718.

Like material will also be found among records of the Palatinates of Chester, Durham and Lancaster in CHES 36; DURH 3 and DURH 9; and PL 23 respectively.

The solicitor was originally most associated with the Court of Chancery, undertaking civil law work relating to trusts, wills and so on, while attorneys were associated with the assizes and common law work. He was sometimes referred to as a **common solicitor** because he would act for anyone provided they paid an agreed fee. It was not until the passing of the Attorneys and Solicitors Act 1729 (2 George II, c 23) that the rapidly developing profession was subjected to some kind of external regulation. This act laid down the rules for admission as either a solicitor or an attorney, adding that attorneys could be admitted as solicitors in Chancery.

Solicitors had to be sworn and admitted by the judges before they could practise in common law courts. C 216, Admission Rolls of Offices and Solicitors, 1596-1875, includes the names of various lord chancellors, masters of the rolls, clerks of the Crown, masters in Chancery, clerks of bankrupts and many others. Readers should note that pieces C 216/22-25, which cover the years 1729 to 1858, are on loan to the Law Society and have to be consulted in the Society's library at 50 Chancery Lane, London WC2A 1SX. Researchers into the careers of solicitors might also like to turn to C 193/141, a register of solicitors struck off in the Court of Chancery between 1905 and 1960.

Somewhat confusingly, the terms 'attorney' and 'solicitor' were often used interchangeably. One person could be described as both. 'Attorney' as a title gradually went out of favour as the term 'solicitor' grew to have connotations of social superiority. However, it would be difficult to pin this process down to a particular period. The modern solicitor, as we would understand the word, came into existence through the Supreme Court of Judicature Act 1873, which amalgamated a number of court officials - the attorney, the solicitor and the proctor (the equivalent officer in ecclesiastical courts) - into a single position.

In contrast to the lengthy history of the solicitor's profession, the modern Bar is largely a Victorian invention. Anyone wishing to become a **barrister** had to join one of the Inns of Court, which, by the Victorian period, were essentially Lincoln's Inn, Gray's Inn, Middle Temple and Inner Temple. Until the twentieth century, it was relatively easy for any male able to pay the fees to join an Inn of Court through which, by eating a set number of dinners and, from 1872, passing a fairly straightforward examination, the prospective barrister would be 'called to the Bar.' By the 1830s, barristers had acquired a monopoly over the right of advocacy in the senior courts and, as an extension of this, had become the only group eligible to provide candidates for appointment to senior judicial positions because only they had the required training as advocates. **Barristers' rolls** from 1868 are in KB 4 (see fig.6).

Until 1919, with the passing of the Sex Disqualification Act, women were barred from practising as solicitors. There was considerable resistance to the opening of the profession to women on the grounds that it was already becoming overcrowded and that to allow women to practise would be to exacerbate the problem. In the event, women were admitted largely despite the opposition of existing practitioners. The first fully qualified female solicitor, Miss Carrie Morrison, a graduate of Girton College, was enrolled in 1922. The first female barrister was Helena Normanton, who was admitted as a member of the Middle Temple in December 1919 and called to the Bar in 1922. Some of her papers are held by the Fawcett Library, London Guildhall University, Old Castle Street, London E1 7NT.

For a study of the developing role of solicitors and barristers, the following piece and classes contain relevant papers: C 27/26, Commission of Inquiry into the Relationship of Various Officers in Chancery, with the nature of their duties and the legality of their fees, 1735; PRO 30/77, Lincoln's Inn Black Books, 1422-1971 [microfilm copies], including admission lists of those called to the bench and bar; TS 4, Admiralty Solicitor: Journals of Proceedings 1828-1865, provides background for claims made by solicitors for costs; and PALA 4, Habeas Corpus Books, 1700-1849, giving details of causes removed to a superior court under the Inferior Courts Act 1623, with names and addresses of attorneys.

Evidence received by the Royal Commission on Legal Services, appointed in 1976 to inquire into the provision of legal services and to suggest desirable changes to the training and structure of the legal professions, can be seen in LCO 19. The Lord Chancellor's Department's main series of registered files in LCO 2 also contains correspondence and papers relating to the legal profession.

The Law Society is the body responsible for overseeing the training of new solicitors, including the setting of suitable examinations; and for ensuring the subsequent good conduct of the persons it admits to its membership. It also once had some responsibilities connected with the administration of legal aid. The Society was initially incorporated in 1831, under the title, 'The Society of Attorneys, Solicitors, Proctors, and others not being Barristers practising in the Courts of Law and Equity in the United Kingdom'. A later Royal Charter of 1903 altered the organization's official title to its present, more concise one. There are some miscellaneous records relating to the Law Society among the records of the Lord Chancellor's Department and, in addition, BT 37/6 includes proceedings before the Law Society, under the provisions of the Solicitors Act 1888, to have bankrupt solicitors struck off the roll. The Law Society retains its own central records.

The counterpart of the Law Society for barristers is the **General Council of the Bar**, established in 1895. It is responsible for maintaining standards among, and investigating complaints against, barristers, as well as representing the profession in its relations with external bodies, including the government. For information about records of the Bar, contact the Bar Council at 3 Bedford Row, London WC1R 4DB.

Useful background reading: Harry Kirk, *Portrait of a Profession: A History of the Solicitor's Profession, 1100 to the Present Day* (Oyez Publishing, 1976) and Raymond Cocks, *Foundations of the Modern Bar* (Sweet & Maxwell, 1983). The printed **Law Lists** and **Alumni Oxon and Cantab** might also help to establish where particular individuals practised.

2.1.7 Judges and Magistrates

A number of the classes mentioned in the section on solicitors and barristers also contain information relating to judges, as judges were - and still are - drawn from existing legal professionals.

From the centrally generated records of the Lord Chancellor's Department, LCO 2 contains many files of correspondence and papers relating generally to judicial matters, such as the appointment of women judges (LCO 2/604) and judicial salaries (LCO 2/6691). The latter subject also crops up among the files of HO 45. For example, HO 45/2153 consists of letters from Victorian county court judges and others discussing the lack of expenses offered to them and bemoaning the pressure of work which prevented them from undertaking other paid work. Preliminary discussions regarding a review of judges' salaries, pensions and allowances in 1948-1949 are preserved among the Treasury's records in T 221/144; and further papers can be found in T 221/359-372.

Researchers seeking documents on the work of judges in particular courts should turn to the section of this guide which deals with the court in question. The surviving records of most of the courts provide some clues to the social make-up of the bench: for example, CRIM 4 includes some commissions of judges for the Central Criminal Court, while DEL 8/1-10 are original commissions for the appointment of judges delegate in the High Court of Delegates. A number of pieces in LCO 12 relate to the appointment of judges to the county courts. HO 68/3 are the original letters patent appointing the lord justices in 1821. While it is of limited historical utility, it is worth braving the heavily soiled packaging to see the virtually undamaged seal attached to the document. Information about judges' attitudes and sentencing practices may be gleaned from the record of court proceedings. Some letterbooks of masters of the rolls, 1873 to 1897 are in J 113. There is also a selection of judges' notebooks, mainly from 1947, in J 130, and there are a few papers of Judge Sir James Miskin, recorder of London from 1975 to 1990, in J 164. The former class is closed for fifty years.

The appointment of **recorders**, **stipendiary magistrates** and **metropolitan police magistrates** was, until 1950, largely the responsibility of the home secretary. A number of Home Office classes contain entry books of considerable relevance. For example, the volumes in HO 60, dealing with the police courts, 1821-1865, include lists of officials appointed to various posts when the courts were established; HO 132, entry books of out-letters to lord lieutenants, mayors and county magistrates, 1872-1873, dealing with issues such as the regulation of fairs, licensing and common lodging houses, the organization of courts and points of law; and HO 159, which deal with magistrates' salaries and fees, 1887-1921. A scanty list of magistrates' names and jurisdictions in 1830 forms HO 94/1. A register of borough Justices of the Peace compiled from the replies to a Home Office circular in 1841 and arranged alphabetically by borough forms HO 90/1. Incidental material on magistrates will also be found in HO 43 and HO 52 (the latter available on microfilm only).

Upon the transfer of responsibility for magistrates to the Lord Chancellor's Department, various files were also transferred from the Home Office and added to the LCD's main series in LCO 2. Other LCO classes contain relevant papers. LCO 34, which is subject to a fifty year closure period, contains records relating to the appointment of Justices of the Peace in the twentieth century. Relatively little is yet available; however, the material which is provides significant information about the social backgrounds, political leanings, previous posts and assessment of general suitability of those put forward for appointment to the magistracy.

Future researchers may well be grateful for the preservation of the record cards of applicants for legal appointments between 1921 and 1979 in LCO 22. This class is closed for seventy-five years because it contains much sensitive personal information about candidates, including summaries of opinions on their suitability for appointment. Class LCO 33 consists of personal and disciplinary files relating to Departmental staff, the judiciary and magistrates, 1915-1984. Again, this is subject to an extended closure period. There is also material concerning Supreme Court staffing matters in J 141.

Other classes which should not be overlooked fall within the Chancery records. Among the miscellaneous Crown Office books in C 193 are many papers on the appointment and work of Justices of the Peace, such as C 193/159 which is a register of borough magistrates, 1938-1966. Also among the Crown Office's records are bundles of fiats for the appointment and removal of JPs from the seventeenth to the twentieth centuries. Records in the Chancery classes are comparatively under-used and for this, as for other areas of research, are likely to yield much valuable information. T 221/283 is a note of the age of retirement of metropolitan stipendiary magistrates between 1921 and the mid 1950s.

Those looking for the magistrates' view of their work may like to consult the notebooks of Sir Robert Blundell in PRO 30/74. Blundell was recorder of Colchester between 1947 and 1949. From 1949 till his death in 1967 he was involved in the stipendiary magistracy in London.

Useful background reading: Thomas Skyrme, *The Changing Image of the Magistracy* (2nd edn, 1983).

2.2 The English Courts of Law

Prior to the twentieth century, many courts were created to deal with the administration of different branches of the law. Some were relatively short-lived and no longer exist, while others still continue to exercise their legal jurisdiction almost unchanged by the passing of time. Still others have been absorbed into, or amalgamated with, other courts to form larger, more widely focused judicial institutions. The history of the law court structure alone could fill a weighty book, so this section can only outline some of the more important points and classes of records which a researcher might find useful.

You should bear in mind that it was court practice to file documents by type so that records about a particular action are likely to be spread over a number of classes, eg affidavits in J 4, pleadings in J 54, orders in J 15 and so on. The drawbacks for researchers were highlighted in 1966 in the *Report of the Committee on Legal Records* (HC, Cmnd 3084, 1966), pp 3-4, known as the 'Denning Report', and since then documents in an action are normally transferred to the PRO in a single dossier. Files relating to the Committee are in PRO 54/153, PRO 54/224-227 and LCO 2/7975-7983.

Many of the courts mentioned below have long histories with surviving records to match. However, the comments are restricted largely to records falling after 1714. One point that you particularly need to note is that, with the exception of a brief period in the 1650s, prior to 1733, most court records were kept in **Latin**, not English. The change to English came about as a result of the Proceedings in Courts of Justice Act 1731, although it was not uncommon for the clerks to make annotations in Latin for some time thereafter, eg *sus* (*supendatur*): let him (or her) be hanged; *cul* (*culpabilis*): guilty.

The legal year was divided into four terms, later known as sittings, covering roughly the following period: Michaelmas (October to December); Hilary (January to March); Easter (April to May); Trinity (June to July). The long vacation ran from the end of Trinity to the beginning of Michaelmas. For fuller information concerning legal chronology see *Handbook of Dates for Students of British History*, edited by C R Cheney (Royal Historical Society Guides and Handbooks, No 4, 1991). Readers wishing to consult this work should refer to the Location Index to Reference Works in the reading or reference rooms.

2.2.1 *Note on Finding Aids in the PRO*

Readers thinking of using court records must be aware that the finding aids for these classes which are provided by the PRO vary widely in age, format and content.

Some are photocopies of poor typescript or manuscript lists prepared when the records in question were transferred to the PRO. Others are manuscript lists contemporaneous with the records themselves, compiled by the court record-keepers as a finding aid to assist in the use of what was documentation relating to current cases. Still others are standard class lists, such as you might have looked at when searching for Home Office or Ministry of Health records. (For an example, see the appendix to this guide: *How to find the correct reference when using HO 45*.)

Eventually it is expected that all the court records held at the PRO will have these standard lists. However, their construction is a massive job, so you would do well to familiarize yourself with the whole range of aids available at an early stage in your work. In a few instances, the finding aids might themselves answer most of your questions.

Most of the contemporary indexes each court created are not available on the open shelves but, for convenience of production, were brought together to form a special class, IND 1, which had to be ordered in the same way as any other document. References to particular IND 1 pieces will be found as appropriate in the following paragraphs. A full catalogue of the IND 1 class (which also explains which classes do not have special indexes) can be found by reference to the Finding Aids Location Index on the open shelves.

No further material is being added to the IND 1 class, and in many instances documents from it are being transferred to associated classes or given a class number of their own, eg Queen's Bench Division cause books, previously in IND 1, now in J 168. This is because the introduction of an automated document production system, coupled with the gradual improvement in class lists and open-plan records storage at Kew, has meant that indexes no longer need to be segregated as formerly.

records of probate, deeds, marriage settlements, household inventories, apprenticeship indentures, contracts, legal opinions, bills of sale and so on. The exhibits include a large quantity of corporate records, especially accounts, relating to commercial disputes. Most researchers engaged in the history of business or commercial law will find something of interest here.

The **Six Clerks** received and filed bills, answers and other papers relating to equity cases before the Court of Chancery; and they kept records in memoranda books from which they could certify to the court the state of proceedings in any case. The six clerks were abolished in 1842 (5 & 6 Victoria, c 103) and replaced by the **Clerks of Records and Writs**. For records of the six clerks' office, see C 11, C 12, and C 13. There are three types of contemporary finding aid for the classes C 5 to C 13 available in IND 1.

The first are the **Bill Books** which note all bills filed and are arranged alphabetically year by year under the first letter of the plaintiff's surname. Though they exist for earlier years, they are most informative for the period after 1713 (IND 1/2142-2151, IND 1/14416-14544).

Second are the **Six Clerks' Cause Books** which are arranged alphabetically by the name of the plaintiff. They give the names of the plaintiffs and defendants in full, and generally offer a good outline of the proceedings in every cause. Each of the six clerks' offices had a set of cause books (IND 1/4105-4207).

Third, the **Clerks in Court books** give the dates of appearances in court and note the names of the solicitors for the parties to each case (IND 1/7388-7525, IND 1/20314-20318). Class C 18, Miscellaneous Proceedings from the Six Clerks' Office, includes court proceedings, affidavits and depositions, many from after 1850. The names of both the plaintiffs and the defendants are given.

The clerks of records and writs kept the Chancery cause books, 1842 to 1880, which are found in C 32. These are particularly useful records of the court's proceedings since for each cause they note the names of all parties to it and their solicitors, together with the dates of appearances made and some information about the records filed in evidence. On the recommendation of the Denning Committee (2.2) later cause books formerly in J 12, have been destroyed apart from certain specimens in J 89.

The **clerks of course**, or **cursitors**, of which there were twenty-four, were responsible for making out all the original writs which were returnable in the court of the King's Bench. These posts were abolished in 1835 (5 & 6 William IV, c 82). The **clerks of the petty bag** made out writs of summons to parliament, pleadings for and against Chancery officials, papers relating to forfeited lands and so on. They were also responsible for enrolling the admission of solicitors, for which see class C 216, Petty Bag Office: Admission Rolls of Officers and Solicitors, 1596-1875.

Attached to the court were **registrars** who were its record-keepers, taking minutes, noting directions issued by the court and so on. For the entry books of decrees and orders kept by the registrars between 1544 and 1875, see class C 33. The **clerk of the Hanaper** controlled the finances of the court with respect to the collection of revenues due and payment of salaries and allowances to its various officers.

Other official posts, many of which were sinecures which were abolished during the mid-nineteenth century, included the clerk of the custodies of lunatics and idiots, the clerk of the presentations, the clerk of the dispensations and faculties, the clerk of the letters patent, the clerk of the Crown (in effect, the lord chancellor's personal assistant), and the examiners in Chancery, who were responsible for examining witnesses and noting their depositions in writing.

From c. 1440, **bills** (i.e. ordinary petitions) and **informations** (i.e. petitions relating to a case involving the Crown or a person or body with rights under the protection of the Crown) are in English. Entry books of petitions presented in Chancery between 1756 and 1858 can be found in C 28. These are arranged by date (for example, C 28/19 is 18 April 1776 to 2 June 1778). C 36 may be a little more useful for finding particular petitions as it is arranged by the first letter of the appellant's name grouped by date (for example, C 36/102 is Hilary 1836 Me to P, where 'Hilary' refers to the second term of the legal year).

The records of Chancery in the PRO are a hugely rich and relatively untapped source for the history of civil law, including family, property and commercial law, from the Middle Ages to almost the present century. The brief description given here barely scratches the surface of the potential of these records. However, you are strongly advised to read as widely as you can before attempting to tackle some of the documents available, particularly for the pre-1733 period.

The Chancery records possess many finding aids, though none are as yet comprehensive and they vary greatly in quality. Information leaflets on Chancery proceedings are available and Professor Henry Horwitz's *Chancery Equity Records and Proceedings; 1600-1800: A guide to documents in the Public Record Office* (PRO Handbooks XXVII, 1995) is a valuable source for research in depth.

2.2.3 Court of the King's (or Queen's) Bench

The King's Bench existed as the highest court of the common law, dealing with matters directly concerning the King or relating to the maintenance of the 'king's peace'. This included actions for trespass and breach of the peace and eventually came to include all kinds of personal action. By the time of the accession of Queen Anne, the court was organized into two parts, the 'crown side', where criminal cases were considered, and the 'plea side' for the consideration of personal actions. The records of the court were divided accordingly. Following the Judicature Act 1873, the court of the King's Bench was abolished and its functions transferred to the Queen's Bench Division of the High Court of Justice.

Records of the Court of the King's Bench are preserved in KB classes. Some are subject to extended periods of closure. They range widely in subject matter, completeness and quality, encompassing affidavits, motions on appeal from inferior courts, records relating to attorneys and officers of the court, depositions, rule books concerning the procedure of the court and much else besides.

Coroners' inquisitions into prisoners who died at the King's Bench Prison between 1746 and 1839 are available in KB 14, while KB 8 consists of official records of 'state trials', principally for treason, including trials of Jacobite rebels of 1715 and 1745 (*see also* 2.1.5).

Amongst the finding aids preserved for King's Bench records are IND 1/6708-6710 which relate to KB 3, Appeals from Inferior Courts, 1876-1906. These are calendars of cases in chronological order, giving the court from which an appeal was being made, the names of the appellant and defendant and a brief note of the outcome.

2.2.4 Court of Common Pleas

The Court of Common Pleas was a central royal court, based in Westminster, which held regular sessions from 1249 till it ceased to exist as a distinct court in 1875. Its jurisdiction was originally to have been virtually unlimited but, by the end of the fourteenth century, it had narrowed largely to civil litigation at common law between the monarch's subjects. In 1875 the court became a division of the High Court of Justice and, in 1881, that division was amalgamated with the Queen's Bench Division.

Until 1837, there were numerous official posts attending the operation of the Court of Common Pleas. They included: the clerk of the warrants, who entered warrants of attorney and enrolled deeds of bargains and sale; the clerk of the seals, who sealed writs; and the clerk of the king's silver, who received monies for fines. In the first year of Victoria's reign, the posts of most of this court's officers were abolished and replaced by five masters. Some of this court's records may be useful for a study of its officials: for example, class CP 4 consists of a bundle of appointments of prothonotaries, filazers and other officers of the court between 1674 and 1831. This is an area where there has been comparatively little research.

Researchers studying debt might wish to investigate a rather special example using CP 16, Index to Debtors and Accountants to the Crown. The records in this class were established in 1839 (under 2 & 3 Victoria, c 11) to protect purchasers of estates by highlighting obligations which might be encumbering them but which might not be easily discoverable. They include details of persons whose estates would be affected by any judgment, statute, recognizance or acceptance of office which would leave them with a debt to the crown. The volumes give details of name, address, title/profession, category of transaction involved, date of the transaction, and the amount of debt, damages or costs owed. From 1879, till the requirement to keep an Index was abolished in 1900, the work was undertaken by the Central Office of the Supreme Court of Judicature.

You can also discover something about **outlawry** in the records of the Court of Common Pleas. If a defendant in an action in the court failed to make an appearance following the first writ served against him or her, the plaintiff could apply to the court for a writ of *exigi facias* as a result of which the sheriff would require the defendant to make a court appearance. If the defendant failed to appear at five successive court sessions, he was

25

'outlawed' and a warrant was issued for his arrest.

If the defendant was then arrested he could pay bail and guarantee his appearance in court, he could be taken into custody pending the grant of a pardon, or he could reverse the outlawry. The most usual way in which outlawry was reversed was by the defendant making a court appearance and paying the plaintiff's costs. Entry books for writs of outlawry, 1821-1870, are to be found in CP 38, with reversals of outlawry, 1737-1860, recorded in CP 39.

Finally, one hazard to watch out for in using Court of Common Pleas papers relating to **ejectment** (i.e. an action for the recovery of property) is the regular appearance of fictitious defendants called 'Richard Roe' or 'John Doe'. The consent rules found in CP 46, Consent Rules in Ejectment 1727-1852, admit the real defendant in an ejectment action in the place of the fictitious ejector Richard Roe, to plead the case.

2.2.5 Exchequer

The Exchequer was established in the reign of Henry I, around 1118. It was a royal court based in London which was concerned principally with calling in debts owed to the monarch. It was divided into two parts, the Upper Exchequer (*scaccarium superius*), which was a court of account in which the royal revenue was managed and questions relating to it were heard, and the Lower Exchequer (*scaccarium inferius*), which actually received and issued money. Until the reign of Henry III, the lord chancellor attended the Exchequer with other principal officers of the king's household; but after this period his place was taken by his clerk, who became the chancellor of the exchequer.

As a court of law, the Exchequer's primary business was to recover land, goods and profits belonging to the crown and to deal with the crown's debtors. It had dealings in both equity and the common law until 1875, when it became a separate division of the High Court of Justice. In 1881 its jurisdiction passed to the Queen's Bench Division.

The records of the Exchequer, which can be found in E classes, are a rich source for the Tudor and Stuart periods, less so for following reigns, though there are some records of the Exchequer as a court of common law for the nineteenth century. These include bills and writs, depositions, minute books and rule books.

2.2.6 Court of Bankruptcy

For information on the Court of Bankruptcy, the records of which are held in B classes, see section on Bankruptcy, Debt and Insolvency (3.1).

2.2.7 High Court of Admiralty

This court seems to have been established during the reign of Edward III. It was concerned with cases involving piracy and spoils, privateering, shipping and merchandise on the seas or overseas. The jurisdiction of the court was divided into two: **Instance** (sometimes known as Ordinary) and **Prize**. The latter was concerned with cases arising out of prizes taken from the enemy in time of war and, from 1660, its business was recorded quite separately from that of the Instance Court.

The Instance Court had both civil and criminal jurisdiction, with the division of the court dealing with cases of murder and piracy sitting at Southwark until the late seventeenth century and at the Old Bailey thereafter. The court's criminal jurisdiction was transferred to the Central Criminal Court in 1834. Records relating to the court's criminal jurisdiction are to be found in class HCA 1, which consists of proceedings of trials for piracy and other crimes committed on the high seas, 1535-1834. Instance records concerning such matters as ship collision, salvage at sea, claims for seamen's wages, etc, are spread over a large number of HCA classes, minute books in HCA 27 and registrars' reports in HCA 54 being particularly noteworthy.

Related items dealing with aspects of the Admiralty's jurisdiction may be found among the records of county courts, the Judicial Committee of the Privy Council, and the High Court of Delegates. Records of the treasury solicitor in TS 13 relate to First and Second World War prize cases.

Under the Judicature Act 1873 the High Court of Admiralty became part of the Probate Divorce and Admiralty Division ('wills, wives and wrecks' as AP Herbert once put it) of the High Court of Justice. In 1970 that Division was renamed the Family Division and its Admiralty jurisdiction was transferred to the Queen's Bench Division in a newly constituted Admiralty court.

2.2.8 High Court of Delegates

This court was established in 1532 to supersede papal jurisdiction in appeals from ecclesiastical courts involving issues such as marriage, legitimacy, tithe disputes, and offences against morality. It also acquired jurisdiction over some maritime cases, principally certain appeals arising from the High Court of Admiralty. The High Court of Delegates was abolished in 1833 (2 & 3 William IV, c 92), when its jurisdiction was transferred to the King in Council. Soon afterwards, by 3 & 4 William IV, c 41, responsibility for such cases was removed to the Judicial Committee of the Privy Council.

The surviving records of the High Court of Delegates (in DEL classes) relate to both ecclesiastical and maritime cases, and many pieces have their own internal indexes. The cause papers, 1600-1834, preserved in DEL 2, are arranged in alphabetical order by the name of the appellant. The dates which appear next to each case are the covering dates for the surviving papers and should not be assumed to be exact in relation to its ending. An index is available of the surnames of the other parties to each case with cross-references to the name of the appellant.

Other important classes are DEL 3, depositions and answers given in particular cases, 1557-1735, and decrees or sentences of the court, 1585-1802, in DEL 5. Among the miscellaneous material gathered in class DEL 8 are the original commissions for the appointment of judges delegate, 1660-1833 (DEL 8/1-32), and repertory books, 1619-1789, giving details of the parties to causes and the judges hearing the actions (DEL 8/70-73). Finally, DEL 10 consists of wills, affidavits and other evidence relating to testamentary appeals from the Prerogative Court of Canterbury and other ecclesiastical courts, 1636-1857.

Useful background reading: G I O Duncan, *The High Court of Delegates* (Cambridge, 1971).

2.2.9 Supreme Court of Judicature

The Supreme Court of Judicature, incorporating a High Court of Justice and a Court of Appeal, was created by consolidation of existing courts under the Supreme Court of Judicature Act 1873 (36 & 37 Victoria, c 66), which came into effect on 1 November 1875. The High Court of Justice received the jurisdictions previously vested in the High Court of Chancery, Court of Common Pleas, Court of Exchequer, High Court of Admiralty, Court of Probate, Court for Divorce and Matrimonial Causes and others. The new High Court was originally established with five Divisions: Chancery, Queen's Bench, Common Pleas, Exchequer, and Probate, Divorce and Admiralty. The Exchequer and Common Pleas Divisions were amalgamated with the Queen's Bench Division in 1881. The London Court of Bankruptcy became the High Court of Justice in Bankruptcy in 1883, and a Crown Court replacing assizes and quarter sessions, became part of the Supreme Court in 1971 and may sit at any place in England and Wales. It also incorporates the Crown Courts established at Liverpool and Manchester in 1956 and the Central Criminal Court (2.2.10) although the latter has retained its name.

The records of the Supreme Court are largely preserved in J classes. Researchers looking for records relating particularly to the 1870s and 1880s are advised to examine the class lists for both the Supreme Court and the older court which was being absorbed, for example, the Court of Chancery (C classes).

The papers of the Supreme Court are extremely wide-ranging. For example, there is a considerable amount of material dealing with the winding-up of companies from the late-nineteenth century (in particular J 13, J 100, J 107, J 119 and J 137); workmen's compensation cases (J 71, J 72); case papers and registers of the Court of Criminal Appeal, which was established in 1907 (J 81, J 82); orders of Divisional Courts (ie, consisting of two or three judges) of the Queen's Bench Division upon appeals from decisions of inferior courts and tribunals, and arising from judicial review of actions of public bodies (J 95); orders, certificates and reports dealing with corruption, illegal practices and the validity of elections (J 85, J 104); affidavits (J4-5, see fig.2); Chancery decrees and orders (J 15); enrolments of change of name by deed poll (J 18); exhibits (J 90); and the work of the Court of Protection and Official Solicitor in dealing with the affairs of minors or those with mental disabilities (J 79, J 80, J 127, J 132, J 136, J 138, and J 156).

The records of the Supreme Court are a rich source for the legal and social history of the nineteenth and twentieth centuries which has till now been relatively little used. Family historians, in particular will be interested in pedigrees preserved among papers of Chancery masters in J 68 and other J classes.

The Denning Report on Legal Records of 1966 (2.2) emphasised the need to improve arrangements for the selection of court records and the disposal of those considered of insufficient value to justify permanent preservation in the PRO. Specimens of classes destroyed in accordance with its recommendations are in J 89.

2.2.10   Central Criminal Court

The Central Criminal Court, better known as the **Old Bailey**, was established by an Act of 1834 (4 & 5 William IV, c 36) for the effective and uniform administration of justice in London and parts of the home counties (i.e. Middlesex, Essex, Kent and Surrey). Its jurisdiction also extends over crimes committed at sea or abroad.

The beginning of a proceeding at the Old Bailey can be found in CRIM 4, Indictments 1834-1957. These documents set out the nature and date of the offence for which trial was taking place, and are generally - though not universally - endorsed with the plea of the accused and the jury's verdict. These records are calendared in CRIM 5, which are arranged by the initial letter of the surnames of persons indicted. As a result these two classes may be of interest to researchers in family history who are looking for possibly criminal ancestors.

Researchers interested in particular twentieth-century cases might also find the calendars of depositions in CRIM 2 of use. Covering the dates 1923 to 1966, these are indexes to cases which were sent up to the Old Bailey from coroners' and magistrates' courts. They include summary details of the hearings which took place in those courts and note the exhibits which accompanied the depositions.

Class CRIM 1, Depositions 1835-1957, are statements given on oath as evidence. The class is closed in part for seventy-five years. Only a selection of depositions has been retained by the PRO. Those relating to trials for murder, sedition, treason, riot, and conspiracy to effect political changes, are permanently preserved, as are others considered to be of a general or historical interest, with a random two per cent of all others. As a result, this class may be of some interest to researchers wishing to undertake a general historical analysis but is likely to be a lucky dip undertaken in vain by anyone looking for a particular individual or material about a particular case (unless it was particularly celebrated: for example, the libel case brought by Oscar Wilde against the Marquis of Queensberry in 1895, the depositions for which are retained as CRIM 1/41/6). The random two per cent sample includes trials for a very wide range of offences such as rape, prizefighting, concealment of birth, sodomy, and attempted suicide. CRIM 1 also includes some pardons.

Some subsidiary documents have been included in CRIM 4, such as jury lists. Further information about the composition of juries can be found in CRIM 6, Court Books 1834-1949, which also give summary details for each trial of offence, plea, verdict, sentence and length of trial. Again, this class is closed in part for seventy-five years.

Details of convicted persons can be found in CRIM 9, which consists of calendars of prisoners, 1855-1949, giving in addition information about magistrates, offences, trial proceedings, verdicts and sentences (see figs. 3-4). Some of these volumes are closed for seventy-five years. In addition, KB 6 contains further nineteenth-century depositions relating to the Central Criminal Court.

As previously stated the, the Central Criminal Court has operated as the Crown Court of the Supreme Court, when sitting in Central London, since 1971.

2.2.11   Other Superior Courts

Records of the **Courts Martial Appeal Court**, established in 1951, are in J 135 and J 152. Corresponding records of Army, Air Force and Naval courts-martial are in WO 71, Air 18 and ADM 156 respectively.

A **Restrictive Practices Court** was established in 1956 to deal with matters brought before it under the Restrictive Trade Practices Act 1956 and later Acts, including the Resale Prices Act 1964 and the Fair Trading Act 1973. It records are in J 154-155.

A **National Industrial Relations Court** was established in 1971, but throughout its existence it was dogged by political controversy, and it was abolished in 1974. Its president's statements, on the opening and closing of the court, and its judgments are in J 111 and J 98 respectively, and are open

reached the Court of Bankruptcy. Surviving papers include: the original letters patent establishing the court in 1630 (PALA 9/6/1); accounts of the fees received by the court's attorneys (PALA 7); bail books giving the names of parties to actions, with an index for the period 1779 to 1836 (PALA 1); and docket books for 1802 to 1849 (PALA 3), naming the parties to, and recording the verdicts given in, individual cases. There are no special indexes preserved in the IND 1 class.

2.2.14   Administrative Tribunals

Administrative tribunals function outside the normal court system and tend to be more accessible, less formal and less expensive. Important tribunals include those deciding disputes concerning employment and social security. In a number of cases a final appeal exists, usually on a point of law, to the High Court. Tribunal members are usually appointed by the minister concerned, and a Council on Tribunals exercises a general supervision over many of them.

Records of administrative tribunals preserved in the PRO include those of the Employment Appeal Tribunal in J 149-150, the Transport Tribunal in AN 80, MT 69, MT 77, MT 80 and MT 145; and Rent Tribunals in HLG 97.

Appeals from Pensions Appeal Tribunals in respect of war disability pensions are in J 96, and records of Pensions Appeal Tribunals themselves are in BF 1-3.

Records of the Council on Tribunals are in BL classes and records of the Committee on Administrative Tribunals and Enquiries, 1955 to 1958, are in LCO 15.

2.3 Court Records Outside the Public Record Office

2.3.1 House of Lords

The House of Lords is at the top of the court hierarchy. It is the final court of appeal for civil cases in the whole of Great Britain (in Scotland since 1707) and for criminal cases in England, Wales and Northern Ireland. With respect to criminal cases, the House of Lords is only willing to consider cases which involve a point of law of general public importance.

Until 1948, the hearing of an appeal usually took place in the House, prior to the hearing of any other business. In 1948 this procedure was altered. Appeals are now heard by the judges in the House, sitting as an Appellate Committee, usually in a group of five, sometimes also including those lay peers who have held high judicial office. Appellate Committees report their decisions to the House which then makes the final Judgment.

Records of the House of Lords' judicial functions, of which its role as a court of appeal is only one, are retained by the House of Lords Record Office. For further information, see Maurice F Bond, *Guide to the Records of Parliament* (HMSO, 1971). At the PRO, there is a single bundle of judgments by the House of Lords in cases on appeal, 1885-1906, in KB 34/1. In addition, LCO 1/46 discusses the hearing of appeals by the House of Lords during the dissolution of parliament, 1885-1886.

Useful background reading: Robert Stevens, *Law and Politics: the House of Lords as a Judicial Body, 1800-1976* (Weidenfeld & Nicolson, London, 1979).

2.3.2 Quarter Sessions and Petty Sessions

From about the fourteenth century, the monarch appointed gentlemen of substantial fortune and good character as '**Justices of the Peace**' (i.e. the king's peace) in order to try offences locally. These JPs (or magistrates) sat in session, with a jury, four times a year, hence the meetings of the JPs' court came to be known as **quarter sessions**. Most crimes could be tried by JPs, with the exception of the most serious offences such as treason and murder which were reserved for the royal judges taking the Assizes.

During the nineteenth century, certain offences were created which could be tried by magistrates sitting in a summary hearing outside the normal quarterly sessions and without a jury. These hearings were known as **petty sessions**. Since the early 1970s the expression 'petty sessions' has been replaced in legislation by '**magistrates courts**'.

Quarter sessions continued till their abolition by the Courts Act 1971 when, together with the assizes, they were replaced by a newly-created Crown Court of the Supreme Court which deals principally with criminal cases, though it also hears appeals from magistrates' courts concerning gaming, betting and licensing. This reorganization arose from the recommendations of the Royal Commission on Assizes and Quarter Sessions, chaired by Lord Beeching, which was appointed in 1966 to report on existing assize and quarter sessions arrangements and suggest reforms. Its report of 1969 can be found in LCO 7/222; and the remainder of LCO 7 consists largely of the evidence that the Commission received.

The records of quarter sessions and petty sessions are public records but, instead of being held at the PRO in London, they are deposited in approved local record offices as being mainly or entirely of local interest. Quarter and petty sessions records are subject to the usual thirty year closure period applied to public records. Researchers wishing to use the records of these courts are advised to contact the appropriate local record office.

This is not to say, however, that there is nothing of interest at the PRO. Until 1992, central government responsibility for the magistrates' courts rested with the Home Office and consequently HO classes are worth investigating. For example, the entry books forming HO 159/1-10 include official forms recording changes to the salaries and fees payable to magistrates and justices' clerks between the late 1880s and 1921. Papers on the reorganization of petty sessional divisions following the Second World War will be found in HO 293. Among these is a file from 1959 (HO 293/21) dealing with the then controversial issue of employing a black Jamaican as a clerk in the Bow Street magistrates' court. Though the chief clerk at the court thought the man's qualifications to be excellent, he explained to the Home Office that he was reluctant to appoint him because of the possible 'repercussions which may ensue from a man of colour...being in a position superior to a number of the staff at court.' A senior Home Office official explained that colour alone could not be allowed to disqualify the applicant and invited the chief clerk to find another reason. The chief clerk eventually produced the argument that white women would be reluctant to give sensitive evidence before a black man, and the Jamaican applicant was rejected.

There are a small number of files appertaining to the relationship between the local courts and the central administration among the records of the Lord Chancellor's Department, particularly in LCO 2.

2.3.3 County Courts

The records of county courts, which came into existence in 1846 to deal with civil law matters, were transferred by the PRO in 1988 to appropriate local record offices. They were formerly preserved under the AK lettercode.

Material dealing with the work of the county courts generally will be found among the records of the Home Office, Treasury and the Lord Chancellor's Department.

2.3.4 Coroners' Courts

Coroners' courts came into existence in 1194. They are courts of inquest, not of trial. Their primary function is to consider the circumstances of violent, sudden, suspicious or unnatural deaths, in order to establish the identity of the deceased, the place and the cause of death. In cases of suspected murder, a coroner is empowered to appoint a jury of between seven and eleven persons. Witnesses are heard and evidence is gathered as in other courts, though the coroners' court has no power to try and convict individuals suspected of murder or other offences relating to a death. Most coroners' inquests in the PRO are on indictment files in ASSI and KB classes. There are also some coroners' inquisitions from the Palatinate of Chester in CHES 18. *Sussex Coroners' Inquests 1558–1603* by R F Hunnisett, (PRO Publications, 1996), is the latest in a good series of examples in print.

Under the Coroners' Act 1988, the coroners' courts also have jurisdiction in the question of the rightful ownership of money, coin, precious metals and other items claimed as treasure trove.

As with the quarter and petty sessions, records of coroners' courts are deposited in the appropriate local record office, to which you should direct enquiries. You should note that papers dealing with deaths are subject to a seventy-five year closure period.

Again, there are a few files to be found, on subjects such as the removal of incompetent coroners, scattered among the records of the Lord Chancellor's Department and the Home Office, between which responsibility for coroners' courts was split.

A useful handbook is *Coroners' Records in England and Wales* by Jeremy Gibson and Colin Rogers (Federation of Family History Societies, 1988).

2.3.5 Ecclesiastical Courts

Researchers looking for records of ecclesiastical courts, such as the Court of Arches, should, in the first instance, seek advice and guidance from the Librarian at Lambeth Palace Library, London SE1 7JU. However, records of the Prerogative Court of Canterbury are in PROB classes, and appeals under the Benefices Act 1898 are in J 142.

2.4 Legal Aid

The modern form of legal aid has its origins in the twentieth-century. Following the passing of the Poor Prisoners' Defence Act 1903, justices were permitted to grant aid to defendants whose cases were being heard in petty sessions. When a legal aid certificate was granted, the solicitor engaged would be paid a relatively small fee, usually around two guineas, which naturally made legal aid work unpopular. The Poor Prisoners' Defence Act 1930 improved the solicitor's financial position a little but, like the earlier act, failed to gain many supporters among justices, with the result that only a very small number of legal aid certificates were granted in comparison to the number of potentially eligible cases heard. Some papers relating to the operation of the Poor Person's Department, which administered this Act, are to be found in J 153.

In the Supreme Court, a form of legal aid was introduced in 1914 to which recourse was more generally made, especially in respect of divorce cases, though the number of cases where assistance was given to the successful completion of proceedings was quite small.

Various problems with the system as originally constituted led to the establishment, in 1919, of a committee chaired by Mr Justice P O Lawrence to consider changes. The Lawrence Committee was eventually approached by the Law Society with a scheme by which it would be responsible for administering legal aid through local committees appointed by the lord chancellor. This scheme was accepted in c.1923 and formed the basis of legal aid administration until after the Second World War.

In 1944 the lord chancellor appointed the Rushcliffe Committee to consider all aspects of legal aid and advice. Its recommendations for a comprehensive system of legal aid operated by the legal profession were embodied in the Legal Aid and Advice Act 1949. Aid based on the new Act was available in the Supreme Court from 1950, including aid for divorce cases, and in the county courts from 1956. The 1949 act permitted solicitors to charge fees for legal aid work which were roughly equivalent to the fees they charged for other work, which greatly increased their willingness to be involved in legal aid assisted cases.

Under the Legal Aid and Advice Act, applications for assistance were made to the area committees of the Law Society, which were instructed to assess the legal merits of the applicant's case. If the area committee was satisfied, the case would then be referred to the appropriate office of the National Assistance Board for investigation of the financial position of the applicant. A grant of a legal aid certificate would depend on the outcome of this investigation. In 1968 the assessment of financial circumstances was transferred to the Supplementary Benefits Commission.

The Legal Aid Act 1974 repealed the 1949 legislation and altered the arrangements for the provision of assistance. Part 1 of the new Act provided for the administration of civil legal aid through the Law Society and the Supplementary Benefits Commission much as before, though in addition it allowed for solicitors to provide legal advice and assistance without applicants needing to apply to the Supplementary Benefits Commission. Part 2 provided for the courts to administer legal aid in criminal cases, with the Supplementary Benefits Commission again having the role of investigating financial circumstances.

Following a further Legal Aid Act, passed in 1988, primary responsibility for the administration of the legal aid scheme passed from the Law Society to the newly-created Legal Aid Board, the members of which are appointed by the lord chancellor. The courts retain some responsibilities for the grant of criminal legal aid.

In 1883 the London Court of Bankruptcy was incorporated into the Supreme Court of Judicature as the High Court of Justice in Bankruptcy. In the same year, provision was made for the official receiver of the Board of Trade to assume control of all a debtor's property in the interests of creditors.

Notices of proceedings in bankruptcy were placed in the *London Gazette*, the official newspaper of the government. A complete set, 1665-1986, is available at the PRO as ZJ 1. Sets may also be available on microfilm or in hard copy in the collections of national and some university libraries.

Records of the London Court of Bankruptcy and its earlier incarnations are to be found in B classes. These include order books relating to petitions against declarations of bankruptcy (B 1), files (B 3 and B 9), various registers of actions, for some of which indexes exist (for example, in B 8), minutes, and gaolers' returns. The majority of the records relate to the nineteenth century, though there are some papers of both the eighteenth and twentieth centuries.

Among records of interest to researchers are BT 40/27, a register of bankruptcies in the London Court of Bankruptcy, 1873-1874, and BT 40/46, a register of bankruptcies in the county courts for 1879. Records of the county courts are generally to be found in local record offices although the London Court of Bankruptcy could hear cases transferred from county courts at creditors' request.

Various classes dealing with the High Court of Justice contain records relating to bankruptcy. These include J 58, warrants for the appointment of attorneys by debtors to confess judgment in the Queen's Bench Division, 1875-1885, for which indexes are available in IND 1/7164-7167. These warrants were in essence a written authority given to a solicitor appointed by the defendant (i.e. the debtor), to concede to the case put by a creditor and agreeing financial terms in settlement of the creditor's claim. For the Court of Common Pleas, CP 16 contains an index to debtors to the Crown, 1839-1878; and CP 48 also includes warrants of attorney to confess judgment. No contemporary indexes exist for CP 48. Warrants of attorney in the plea side of the King's Bench are preserved in KB 128.

Among the records of the Lord Chancellor's Department, class LCO 28 consists of the registers, 1854-1964, of petitions for protection from process which were kept by the Registry of County Court Judgments, an office which was established by the County Courts Act 1852. The Registry's duties ceased in 1861, following a change in practice as regards insolvent debtors, but were resumed in 1883 in respect of debtors in bankruptcy under the Bankruptcy Act 1883. Each register gives the petitioner's name, address and occupation, with details of the court and debt involved in each case. They are arranged by date and initial letter of the surname: for example, LCO 28/3 is the register for 1924 to 1955, letter C.

3.1.2 Central Government Responsibility

For files concerned with central government policy and legislation, see LCO 2, the main class of registered files for the Lord Chancellor's Department. There are also a small number of related files in LCO 1, such as LCO 1/15 which consists largely of memoranda produced by officials and judges on the unsatisfactory working of sections 122 and others of the Bankruptcy Act 1883. This file provides some useful papers outlining the pitfalls of the Bankruptcy Acts in general, and also highlights the problems which could be caused by the poor drafting of legislation. LCO 1/53 includes papers concerning the amalgamation of the Insolvent Debtors Court with the Court of Bankruptcy.

The Board of Trade's Bankruptcy Department was established in 1883 when the Bankruptcy Act transferred to the Board the administrative functions formerly exercised by the courts. It was responsible for the investigation, regulation and administration of all insolvencies of individuals and firms following the making of a Receiving Order by a court in England or Wales. Class BT 37 contains papers concerned with general policy and precedent in this area. Related registers and indexes for the period to 1902 can be found in BT 38. Registers of deeds of arrangement which give the name of the debtor and trustee, the value of the debtors' estate and his liabilities, and details of the type of deed involved (e.g. an assignment of real and personal estate upon trust for the benefit of creditors and release of the debtor) for the years 1888 to 1947 are in BT 39. Perhaps the most useful aspect of these registers for family historians is that they include the addresses of debtors.

Records relating to the work of the Board of Trade's Bankruptcy Department outside the High Court can be found in BT 221. These include audits of assets, assignment and official releases of trustees and case papers. There are no special indexes to this class.

3.1.3 The Official Receiver

The Board of Trade was empowered to establish an official receiver of debtors' estates by sections 66-71 of the Bankruptcy Act 1883. BT 289/8 is a register of the official receivers appointed between 1907 and 1953, arranged by county court, and including dates of resignation or death. It may have some limited use as a cross-reference facility for researchers trying to determine which official's initials are appended to particular documents. The official receiver was, in addition, to have responsibility for investigating the conduct of debtors and assisting in the prosecution of fraudulent debtors.

BT 293 contains the official receivers' registers of all persons served with petitions for bankruptcy in both the High Court and county courts between 1884 and 1923. It is important to note that not every petition resulted in a bankruptcy. The registers are arranged alphabetically and chronologically and give the following information for each petition: name, address and occupation; name of court; date of filing petition and receiving order; date of first public examination of petitioner; date of adjudication of the case; details of trustee appointed; date of payments with rate of dividend; and the date of discharge. While not in themselves particularly revealing, these registers can be used as an index to BT 226, papers of the High Court relating to bankruptcy cases. The 'distinctive numbers' given in the registers in BT 293 are the same as the case numbers of BT 226. These case numbers are noted in the class list.

The High Court papers in BT 226 deal with bankruptcy applications put to the court by the official receiver and with public examinations of individuals. For the period 1891 to 1914, the records have been preserved in their entirety. For 1915 to c.1930, the files are only a random selection. From then onwards, the files have been selected to form a representative sample with infamous and unusual cases also permanently preserved. Most of the files largely follow the pattern of BT 226/2507, the case of Arthur Valentine Smeeton, a City of London costume and blouse manufacturer.

Smeeton's own statement of evidence was that he set up business in 1880 and was very successful at first. A fire at his premises in 1904 caused £25,000 damage, destroying the new season's stock and leaving him financially embarrassed as he was under-insured by £3,000. At this point he had begun speculating on the Stock Exchange to try to recoup his losses, but had no talent for it. He was soon plunged into very serious debt. A bound volume contains a chronological record of the proceedings of the case, beginning 19 August 1908, when a receiving order was made on the petition of the debtor, and ending on 1 September 1910 when Smeeton's trustee was released from his duties. It records the appointment of a solicitor, accountant, trustee and committee of inspection; and the dispersal of Smeeton's estate, i.e. his stock and property, to settle his debts. A bundle of supporting evidence includes a list of Smeeton's unsecured creditors with the amounts and reasons for the debts, such as supply or conveyance of goods; his fully secured creditors, in this case insurance companies; and his semi-secured creditors. It also includes a description of Smeeton's assets, which included a motor car worth £100, and monies owing to him.

BT 37/4 consists of more general and discursive papers emanating from the official receivers' branch on such subjects as expenses incurred in the administration of estates, instructions for the public examination of debtors, the desirability of salaried official receivers, and the need to establish an inspectorate. One file (B1316/1887) in the piece is an examination of the reasons for failed prosecutions under the Debtors' Act in the years 1884, 1885 and 1886. Around nineteen per cent of cases had been acquitted by juries in these years. The comments of various Board of Trade and other officials are revealing of the kinds of class prejudices evident in the ranks of the Civil Service of the time. One noted that

> A large number of cases...owed their failure entirely either to the ignorance and stupidity of the Jury and their consequent inability to understand the facts submitted to them - or to their feelings of sympathy with the prisoner. As an instance of this, the OR at Gloucester reports in the case of Harry Villar-Cheltenham 15/84 'I am quite sure that the Common Jury failed to grasp or understand the evidence. One had only to look at the class of men they were to understand this. I was informed that the foreman was an ostler, and that two others had themselves failed.'

Amongst other records of the official receivers' work in the early twentieth century is an incomplete set of ledgers, covering both the High Court and the county courts, containing records of the realization and distribution of the assets of bankrupt individuals (BT 294). These are arranged alphabetically, giving the date, particulars of the estate, payments and receipts and the final balance. For the second half of the twentieth century, some establishment records survive in BT 296, particularly for the official receivers' provincial offices.

3.1.4 The Imprisonment of Debtors in London

At the beginning of the nineteenth century, there were three debtors' prisons in London. The **Fleet Prison** stood on the banks of the Fleet River from the Middle Ages to 1842. The **Marshalsea Prison**, originally a branch of the Court of the Verge and Marshal, the disciplinary branch of the medieval royal household, was, by the eighteenth century, situated next to the **Queen's (or King's) Bench Prison** in Southwark. Some of the individuals confined within it were debtors, though the Marshalsea was also used to hold smugglers, Admiralty prisoners detained after court martial, persons guilty of contempt of court, and others. It was closed in 1842, upon its merger with the Fleet and Queen's Bench Prisons to form the **Queen's Prison**, which was itself closed in 1862. Thereafter, no special debtors' prison existed.

The Debtors Act 1869 abolished imprisonment for debt except for debtors to the crown, defaulting trustees or solicitors, or 'judgment debtors' (i.e. those able to pay, but refusing to do so).

PRIS 1 consists of commitment books for the Fleet Prison, 1685 to 1842. There are gaps as some volumes were destroyed during the Gordon Riots in 1780. Condensed versions of the prison commitment books can be found in PRIS 10/21-26, which fill the gap in the main series for the years 1769 to 1778. Other sources provide some information for further gaps, but commitments for 1729-1733 and 1748-1769 have proved to be irrecoverable. PRIS 10/136-137B relate to the recapture of prisoners who were released from the Fleet and King's Bench Prisons by participants in the Gordon Riots.

The persons recorded in the Fleet Prison commitment books are those who were unable to stand bail for themselves and were committed until bail was paid. They were held in the Fleet at the expense of their creditors. Each entry in the register gives the name of the person committed with the date and name of the justice ordering the committal, and the charge against the committed person. Some entries have marginal notes indicating the date of discharge or date of death if this occurred whilst the debtor was still committed. PRIS 1/1A-4 are written in Latin; thereafter the records are in English, in conformity to the provisions of the Proceedings in Courts of Justice Act 1731. Indexes exist to all the volumes except PRIS 1/3.

Commitments files, including writs of *habeas corpus* from justices to the sheriffs detaining debtors, confirmations of arrest issued by sheriffs, and details of debtors' discharge of bail by admission to the Fleet Prison, can be found in PRIS 2 for the period 1758 to 1842. Case numbers appear on the papers in these bundles, which can be cross-referenced to the commitment books in PRIS 1. For example, information on cases mentioned in PRIS 2/108, Fleet Prison commitments file for July 1812 to January 1813 (numbers 15,178 to 15,450), will also be found in PRIS 1/27, Fleet Prison commitment book, June 1812 to September 1813.

Some discharges of debtors from the Fleet Prison, 1775-1842, can be traced in PRIS 3. These discharge warrants, addressed to the warders of the prison have, in some cases, been annotated with the commitment book entry number to be found in PRIS 1. Debtors were released when the debt was paid (often through the intervention of charity); if the prisoner was freed in accordance with an Insolvent Debtors' Act; or once the plaintiff's opportunity to render a case against the defendant had expired. The information in PRIS 3 is, to some extent, replicated in PRIS 10/49-57, which have the advantage of being indexed. However, these latter volumes also cover the period 1734-1743. PRIS 10/157 is a commitment and discharge book for the Fleet Prison covering an even earlier period, 1697-1702.

Commitment books for 1747 to 1862 for the King's (or Queen's) Bench Prison, and its replacement, the Queen's Prison, similar to those for the Fleet Prison in PRIS 1, are held as PRIS 4. Summaries of the details in these books are in the abstract books in PRIS 5. Though this latter set of volumes are often inferior copies, they do have the advantage of being indexed, which enables the information recorded here to be cross-referenced to the warrants of discharge for the King's Bench Prison in PRIS 7.

The execution books in PRIS 8 record payments of debt and discharge of debtors from the King's Bench, and later Queen's, Prison. Unfortunately, not all debtors were discharged from the King's Bench Prison before death struck. Coroners' inquisitions on dead prisoners from this prison, for the years 1746-1750 and 1771-1839, can be found in KB 14.

Few records of the Marshalsea exist. PRIS 11/1-13 consist of commitment books, 1811 to 1842, giving the names of debtors, their creditors and attorneys, with the sums involved in their cases.

There are few records which relate solely to the Queen's Prison. PRIS 9/1 and PRIS 9/2 are the donation books of prison charities, including legacies and gifts of food and clothing to the neediest prisoners, with details of the donor. The copy letter books of Captain John Hudson, governor of the prison between 1843 and 1862, and the keeper's daily journals in PRIS 9/6-19 provide some insight into the workings of the prison in its everyday life.

An equally valuable set of records for understanding life within the Queen's Prison, and no doubt the earlier debtors' prisons too, is held in PRIS 6. These volumes give important details about the internal discipline of the prison. Offences, which included drunkenness, threatening behaviour, consorting with prostitutes, slander and brawling, were described by the reporting officer, with supporting statements of witnesses appended and the decision of the prison governor noted. Charges were sometimes dismissed, but those found guilty could be either cautioned or delivered to the 'strongroom' for a period of confinement.

Of some interest to family, as well as social, historians might be class RG 7, containing unauthenticated registers relating to clandestine marriages taking place in the Fleet and other debtors' prisons between c.1667 and c.1777. These registers, some of which have internal indexes, were generally kept by the ministers or clerks who performed the marriages or by the landlords of the houses in which the ceremonies took place. A few were compiled by self-appointed record-keepers. The information in these volumes has been distilled into recently-compiled indexes of parishes, grooms' names and brides' names, which also note the occupation of the groom. These modern indexes are available as part of the class list at the PRO.

Accounts relating to building works at the debtors' prisons can be found in WORK 5/74-103. Miscellaneous papers relating to debtors will also be found in PCOM 9.

3.1.5 Imprisonment of Debtors outside London

Of course, London was not the only area of the country in which debtors were imprisoned. Researchers should, however, turn first to their local record office for sources. The *London Gazettes* at Kew in ZJ 1 may also be assistance.

Arguably the most useful source available is a register of debtors received into Lincolnshire county gaol between 1810 and 1822, preserved as PCOM 2/309. This register, which appears to be a fair copy possibly written in 1822, gives details of around 1200 prisoners, including their names, their debts and the courts from which they came. Analysis of this register provides a useful comparison to the metropolitan situation. The B6 class also includes registers of petitions of country prisoners.

As with many other areas discussed in this guide, it is worth consulting the Home Office class HO 45. One example of a relevant file is HO 45/775. This contains a number of fascinating descriptions of conditions in the debtors' prison in Birmingham in the 1840s. A local notable, Mr Weale, visited the prison in December 1843 and was so horrified by the 'den of wretchedness' that he found that he wrote to the home secretary in protest. The debtors' prison was, he explained, formerly an ordinary dwelling house. Twenty-two 'poor creatures', including one woman, were provided with straw bedding and a ten inch wide sleeping space. The Recorder of Birmingham, Matthew Davenport Hill, subsequently reported that the prison was infested with rats. An inspection by John Perry, Inspector of Prisons, in January 1844 confirmed that the debtors' prison was in an unacceptably poor condition. His report, which can be found in HO 45/775, also commented on the cruelty of the inmate subculture and the initiation ceremonies through which new inmates were put by their longer-serving fellows. These descriptions are particularly useful because they lack the sensationalism of many of examples of the genre which can be found in Victorian publications.

3.1.6 Reviews of the Law of Bankruptcy

Various committees have considered and commented on the law as it affects bankruptcy and insolvency. The Bankruptcy Law Amendment Committee, chaired by Judge Blagden, was appointed by the president of the Board of Trade in October 1955 to consider whether the Bankruptcy Acts 1914 and 1926 needed amendment. It reported in 1957, and a small number of the committee's papers, including some correspondence and minutes of

before parliament was a wife's adultery and it was, in essence, a measure designed to protect the property rights of legitimate offspring. It was an expensive process and there tended to be only three or four cases a year. The House of Lords Record Office is the main repository for private divorce acts, but a few examples will be found in C 89 and C 204.

There were other ways of breaking a marriage, including wife sale, which was comparatively rare, and simple separation or desertion, which was doubtless common though unquantifiable. However, it is considerably more difficult to trace evidence of these kinds of severances. Poor law records, which tend to be held by local record offices, may offer the richest sources.

The Matrimonial Causes Act, which came into force in 1858, was designed to clarify the laws surrounding marriage and separation which had become extremely confused over time. It allowed for the establishment of a civil court for hearing divorce and matrimonial causes which took over the jurisdiction of the ecclesiastical courts. Appeal was to the House of Lords. The permissible basis for divorce remained largely unchanged, with husbands having the right to sue for divorce on the grounds of a wife's adultery alone, whilst a wife had to prove the husband guilty of bigamy, bestiality, sodomy or other offence in addition to adulterous behaviour. A wife was not permitted to sue for divorce on the grounds of a husband's adultery alone till 1925. However, perhaps the most significant piece of twentieth century legislation was the Divorce Reform Act 1969 which made the irretrievable breakdown of marriage the only grounds for divorce. Breakdown could be shown to have occurred if there was adultery, unreasonable behaviour, desertion for at least two years or separation for at least five.

The jurisdiction of the civil court for hearing divorce and matrimonial cases was transferred to the Supreme Court of Judicature in 1875, where it became part of the Probate, Divorce and Admiralty Division of the High Court of Justice. This was renamed the Family Division in 1970. Classes J 77 and J 78 are a rich source of information on divorce between 1858 and c.1958. J 77 includes files of papers arising from petitions for divorce and judicial separation, sometimes incorporating original petitions stating the grounds for divorce, and also court minutes. These files are indexed by the names of the parties in the volumes comprising J 78. It should be noted that after 1937 only a representative selection/samples of files are being preserved. Of less direct interest to family historians, but of great potential interest to other researchers, is class J 132, Supreme Court of Judicature, Official Solicitor: Divorce Papers, 1938-1973. These records consist of a random two per cent sample of cases where the Official Solicitor was involved, acting on behalf of an interested party, and are all presently subject to an extended closure period.

For those seeking more general insight into the creation and maintenance of divorce law, the registers in TS 29 contain brief descriptions of matrimonial cases in which the procurator general had decided that a decree nisi should not be made absolute, while LCO 2 includes some useful papers on the provision of legal aid for matrimonial cases and BC 1 and BC 2 include recent Law Commission reports and papers proposing reforms to the law. The dedicated researcher may also find something of interest in the Home Office records, which include such interesting sidelights on the subject as the case of a woman granted a divorce in 1954 on the grounds that her husband had been convicted of murder (HO 291/137).

Useful background reading: Lawrence Stone, *The Road to Divorce in England, 1530-1987* (Oxford University Press, 1990).

3.3 Adoption

Before the passing of an Adoption Act in the 1920s, there was no legal form of adoption in England and Wales. The term 'adoption' was sometimes used to describe the arrangements made between poor families and wealthier childless couples for the transfer of children; and it was certainly the case that charitable societies for the rescue of destitute children, such as Dr Barnardo's and the Church of England Waifs and Strays Society, would describe the placing of children with families in the UK or elsewhere in the Commonwealth as adoption. However, the common law did not recognize that any transfer of a father's rights over his children to another person was possible. One result of this is the absence of any systematic records relating to the placing of children with families in the nineteenth century.

Following the First World War, the minds of many politicians and charity workers were focused on the plight of the fatherless child and the unmarried mother. Recognizing some of the adverse social stresses which the war had created, the government established the Hopkinson Committee in 1920 to consider whether legal adoption was advisable in England and Wales and if so, what form it should take. There was overwhelming support for the principle of adoption, but more difficulties were raised over its form.

Eventually a new committee, the Tomlin Committee, was appointed in an attempt to find a consensus, and it produced a draft Bill which formed the basis of the Adoption Act 1926. This Act deprived the natural parents of a child being put forward for adoption of any future rights over the child, passing them to the adoptive parents. However, a distinction between natural and adopted children remained, as an adopted child did not automatically become a legitimate heir of its adoptive parents until further changes to the law in 1949.

Researchers seeking information on individual adoptions should turn to the Office of Population Censuses and Surveys at St Catherine's House, 10 Kingsway, London WC2B 6JP. The adoption records which it keeps begin on 1 January 1927. However, the indexes for adoption certificates show only the adoptive name and the names of the adopting parents, and do not show the name before adoption.

There are few records at the PRO of great relevance to a study of adoption. The main series of registered papers for the Lord Chancellor's Department and the Home Office, LCO 2 and HO 45 respectively, include some files on the background to adoption legislation. Records of the Home Office Children's Department relating to the development of policy on adoption can be found in BN 29, particularly BN 29/22-43, which are files on the Adoption Bill 1957 and Adoption (Consolidation) Bill 1958. PIN 11, part of the Ministry of Pensions records, includes some incidental material on adoption.

Among the correspondence and papers of the General Register Office on the registration of births, marriages and deaths, preserved as RG 48, there are further files on adoption dating from 1926 onwards.

The Official Solicitor's records include a small number of files relating to work in connection with adoption, dating from the 1960s. These papers, in class J 138, are closed for seventy-five years.

3.4   Defamation, Libel and Slander

Defamation is the publication of a statement which tends to damage the good reputation which a person has among reasonable members of society generally, or which makes them ostracize the person defamed. In order to constitute a **tort** (i.e. a civil wrong or injury for which an action for damages may be brought), the statement must be false, the words used in their ordinary meaning must be capable of bearing a defamatory meaning and the statement must be published to at least one other person besides the person allegedly defamed.

The form of publication determines whether the act of defamation is libel or slander. **Slander** is a defamatory statement made in a transitory medium, generally speech, while **libel** is the publication of a defamatory statement in a permanent form, such as print, pictures and writing (see frontispiece). In addition, television broadcasting (under the Defamation Act 1952), theatre performances (under the Theatres Act 1968) and film have been interpreted for these purposes as a permanent medium. Libel may be a criminal offence as well as a tort in the civil law. However, it is significant that, in the twentieth century, the vast majority of actions for libel are brought under the civil rather than the criminal law.

A statute making defamation against judges or nobles a criminal offence, *De scandalum magnatum* (slander of magnates), was enacted during the reign of Edward I in 1275. Similar measures were enacted in later reigns. These acts were generally intended to prevent a loss of confidence in government and were largely used as a political weapon. From its establishment in 1488 to its abolition in 1641, Star Chamber was the main vehicle for enforcing the law against those accused of seditious libel, i.e. attempting to undermine the goverment's authority or threaten state security by publishing defamatory statements. The truth of a defamatory statement was no defence, nor did the death of the person libelled stop a case in Star Chamber.

Following the Restoration, the jurisdiction of Star Chamber was inherited by the Court of King's Bench. Diligent researchers may, therefore, find material of interest in KB and TS classes at the PRO. The eighteenth century saw a number of overtly political prosecutions in the Court of King's Bench for criminal libel, ie where it is blasphemous, obscene or seditious, most notably of John Wilkes in 1763 and Thomas Paine in 1792. However, by the time Victoria ascended the throne, such prosecutions for political libel had virtually ended.

It was not until the sixteenth century that the common law courts began to develop a civil action for slander, in which the main concern was the reputation of the private individual. The common law courts were soon in danger of being overwhelmed by actions for slander brought by ordinary subjects. Therefore, in order to bring a measure of control, the judges restricted the action of slander to a small number of well-settled categories: imputation of crime, imputation of incompetence in a trade or profession or imputation of certain diseases, such as venereal disease. Unlike in the criminal charge of libel, the truthfulness of the defamatory statement was from the first a defence to a civil action for libel.

As in so many other areas, the nineteenth century saw movement toward reform of the law of defamation and libel. A Select Committee of the House of Lords was appointed in 1843 to consider and recommend changes to the existing law. Its recommendations formed the basis for the Libel Act enacted in the same year. The most significant change made by this law was that the truthfulness of a defamatory statement could be a defence against a criminal prosecution for libel if it could also be shown that the publication of the statement was for the public benefit. Two later, significant pieces of legislation were the Law of Libel Amendment Act 1888, which somewhat altered the circumstances under which newspapers could be prosecuted for libel, and the Defamation Act 1952.

The Defamation Act 1952 was built upon the recommendations of the Committee on the Law of Defamation, chaired by Lord Porter. Among its other members was E M Forster. This Committee was appointed in 1939, suspended on the outbreak of war, and resumed in 1945. Papers relating to the work of this Committee can be found in LCO 2/3058-3068. The file preserved as LCO 2/3058 discusses a failed Bill on libel law in 1939 which prompted the creation of the Committee. It includes correspondence and memoranda dealing with the practical aspects of the Committee's establishment and its disruption by the Second World War. There is a great deal of typescript evidence, both submitted and minutes of oral evidence, given by interested parties. Among the most interesting is evidence given by representatives of newspaper and book publishing businesses which will be found in LCO 2/3064. The report of the Porter Committee (for which see LCO 2/4118) was published in 1948.

Papers discussing the merits of the Defamation Bill arising from the report are preserved as LCO 2/4858-4861; and notes on the amendments to the Bill as it went through Committee Stage in the House of Commons can be found in LCO 2/5578.

In 1971 the lord chancellor and the lord advocate (the lord chancellor's counterpart in Scotland) appointed a Committee, chaired by Mr Justice Faulks, to consider the working of the Defamation Act 1952, and recommend whether any changes were needed to the law, practice and procedures relating to actions for defamation. Files containing committee working papers, written submissions, shorthand transcripts of the oral evidence of witnesses and drafts of the Committee's report are held as LCO 13. The vast majority of the pieces are, at the time of writing, closed under the thirty year rule.

On a related subject, records of a committee which was appointed in 1970 to consider whether legislation was needed to protect the individual against intrusions into privacy, are preserved as HO 264. These records are presently closed to researchers until 2001.

There are many other scattered papers dealing with defamation in the records of the Lord Chancellor's Department and, to a limited degree, the Home Office. Researchers looking for information on individual actions should, of course, consult the records of the appropriate court.

Chapter 4: CRIME DETECTION

4.1   Pre-Nineteenth Century Policing

Traditionally, before the nineteenth century, a number of bodies had been concerned with policing the local community with a view to detecting and deterring crime. The bulk of responsibility rested on the parish authorities. The highest authority in each locality was the **Justice of the Peace (JP)** whose duty it was to grant search warrants and arrest warrants, undertake preliminary investigations into serious crimes, give judgment in cases of petty crime, initiate investigation of crimes and undertake a wide range of local administrative duties relating to public order and so on.

The JP's subordinate was the unpaid **parish constable** who, among other duties, organized the **watch and ward**, a body of local men appointed: to be vigilant during the hours of darkness (the watch) and similarly during the day (the ward); to take charge of any persons accused of wrongdoing by the watch and ward or by any other resident of the parish; and to see that the accused were forwarded as appropriate to a court of law.

This system of local policing had its problems. Parishioners were fully aware that the constable could find himself seriously financially disadvantaged as a result of holding the office, for it disrupted his normal work activities and often entailed extra expenses not fully reimbursed through the permitted fees. As a result, the office was viewed with some lack of enthusiasm. The small geographical area of the parish, beyond the boundaries of which the constable had no jurisdiction, also limited the value of the system. However, recent research has suggested that parish policing may have been much more effective than had been previously thought.[1]

Records of the system of parish policing have survived only patchily. They tend to be found amongst the collections of parish records generally deposited in local authority record offices. For example, the records of New Romney parish in Kent, now in the custody of the Centre for Kentish Studies, include a warrant issued to the constable of the parish in 1719 for the apprehension of a James Tipping.[2]

---

[1] See Joan R Kent, *The English Village Constable 1580-1642: A Social and Administrative Study* (Clarendon Press, Oxford, 1986).
[2] Centre for Kentish Studies, reference P309/10/1.

The efficiency of parish policing in the early nineteenth century was central to the inquiries of the Royal Commission appointed to Inquire as to the Best Means of Establishing an Efficient Constabulary Force, which reported in 1839. Pieces HO 73/5-9 consist of evidential returns sent to the Commission by local authorities between 1836 and 1839. The form used to solicit information had thirty-four questions and, as with all surveys, the level of response was varied, from the barest minimum possible to extremely full descriptions of the local situation. Nevertheless, these returns provide a considerable quantity of detailed information about the system and experience of law and order in provincial parishes before the creation of more formal, centralized policing, including estimates of the number of felonies and misdemeanours committed in the previous twelve months, the existence of vagrants' lodging houses and beer houses, the frequency of malicious damage, cattle wounding and arson, any difficulties in maintaining order on the roads and whether the parish had any voluntary organizations for the suppression of vagrancy. They would be useful to any researcher interested in issues such as the incidence of machine-breaking and politically-motivated disturbances in the 1830s, incendiarism, and the distribution and accessibility of local Justices of the Peace.

HO 73/71 is the comment of Mr Freeland, a Chichester magistrate, on the state of the rural police in 1837. Like some of the officials completing the formal return, Mr Freeland supported the existing system of policing based on parishes, but suggested that poor law guardians should be given the power to pay police constables. The Royal Commission's report was subsequently published in the series of Sessional Papers of the House of Commons (169, 1839, XIX, I) and may be seen at the PRO on microfilm.

The process of law enforcement through the parish remained virtually unchanged until the mid-eighteenth century, when the development of more urban areas, in particular the rapid growth of the metropolis, began to show the inadequacies of a very localized, unpaid form of policing. From about 1735, many areas began to seek private acts of parliament which would permit them to raise funds through the rates to pay for more thorough schemes by which crime might be better deterred and detected. The fact that they could now levy a rate enabled parish authorities to pay for full-time constables and other law enforcement officers who could patrol the area more regularly, who would be properly accountable and who would be better able to co-operate with the authorities of neighbouring parishes.

This was regarded as a great step forward in controlling crime and became a relatively widespread phenomenon, though its spread was piecemeal as each act of parliament had to be separately pursued.

Acts of 1842 and 1850 had a more general impact on the organization of policing. The first of these, the Parish Constables Act 1842 (5 & 6 Victoria, c 109) empowered quarter sessions to build lock-ups and made compulsory the appointment of a superintending constable, paid for from the county rates, to take charge of the lock-up and supervize the unpaid parish constables. The latter act (13 & 14 Victoria, c 20) allowed quarter sessions to appoint paid officers to supervize constables on the basis of the petty sessional divisions.

From the mid-eighteenth century, the activities of the parish authorities in some areas were supplemented by **associations for the prosecution of felons**. These organizations were formed by groups of local property-owners, concerned at the level of crimes committed against themselves and their possessions, who would create a fund which would pay for the discovery and prosecution of offenders. Associations would usually work with the parish constable, helping to make his role more effective by enlarging the resources at his disposal, though very occasionally they employed their own 'police' staff, and also employed Bow Street Runners (4.2.1).

As a form of law enforcement agency, the associations for the prosecution of felons were most active between c.1770 and c.1850. Estimates of the total number of active organizations range from 750 to over 4000, depending on the sources used to make the calculation.[3] HO 73/5-9, the local returns to the royal commission on efficient policing mentioned earlier, include details of associations for the prosecution of felons where these existed in the 1830s. In the end, their purpose for existence was largely undermined by government directives insisting on the creation of publicly-funded police forces. Records relating to these societies are generally to be found in local record offices. For example, Wiltshire Record Office holds minutes

---

[3]. David Philips, 'Good Men to Associate and Bad Men to Conspire: Associations for the Prosecution of Felons in England, 1760-1860' in *Policing and Prosecution in Britain, 1750-1850,* (ed) D Hay and F Snyder (Clarendon Press, Oxford, 1989). This article gives a fuller history of the Associations than is possible here and contains a useful appendix listing the names of Associations and their dates of establishment.

and accounts, 1787-1887, of the Devizes Society for the Prosecution of Felons.[4]

4.2 Policing the Metropolis

4.2.1 Bow Street Runners

By the end of the eighteenth century, there had been all manner of local initiatives, arising from local government authorities rather than private organizations, which had altered the old system of parish policing. Among these, one of the most significant was the creation, in 1749, of the **'Bow Street Runners'**. The Runners were the first salaried police officers in London, able to cross the parish boundaries in pursuit of offenders. At first, arrangements (and funding) were fairly casual, but gradually they became more systematized so that, by 1782, the officers had become recognized as the Foot Patrol. They were joined by a Horse Patrol, to control highway robbery, in 1805. Other complementary patrols were established over time, providing precedents and experience which would prove useful to Sir Robert Peel in his desire to create an effective police force for the metropolis.

Peel was home secretary during most of the 1820s. A supporter of penal reform, he believed that an essential corollary was the establishment of a modern policing service which could eliminate both the petty corruptions possible under existing practices and the need to call upon the army to put down instances of civil disorder, which had proved so damaging in the past as, for example, in the Peterloo Massacre of 1817. Peel had previously been involved in the creation of an Irish police force. He had allies, such as the Duke of Wellington, but he also faced widespread opposition to the plan he proposed, which was this: the establishment of a salaried, uniformed, civilian force of officers dedicated to policing the metropolis and paid for by those householders in the metropolitan area who already paid the poor rate.

After a decade of agitation and opposition, during which the threat to freedom and liberty presented by the proposed police force was fiercely debated, the **Metropolitan Police Act** was finally passed in 1829, to come into operation in 1830, covering an area of seven miles radius from Charing

---

[4]. Wiltshire Record Office, County Hall, Trowbridge BA14 8JG. Ref: 1553.

Cross. Within a year, seventeen police divisions had been established centred on the following places: Westminster (A), Chelsea (B), Mayfair and Soho (C), Marylebone (D), Holborn (E), Kensington (F), King's Cross (G), Stepney (H), West Ham (K), Lambeth (L), Southwark (M), Islington (N), Peckham (P), Greenwich (R), Hampstead (S), Hammersmith (T) and Wandsworth (V). Clapham (W), Willesden (X) and Holloway (Y) were added in 1865; Bethnal Green (J) was added in 1886, bringing the total number of divisions to twenty-one. MEPO 15/14 maps the Metropolitan Police Districts in 1914.

The **Bow Street Horse Patrol** was absorbed into the Metropolitan Police in 1836, as was the Foot Patrol in 1839 following the Metropolitan Police Act of that year which also extended the force's district to a fifteen mile radius from Charing Cross. Among the records of the Metropolitan Police, held in the MEPO classes at the PRO, is MEPO 2/25 which includes some papers, 1827-1845, relating to the operation of the Bow Street Horse Patrol and the Mounted Branch of the Metropolitan Police, such as correspondence on the allowances payable for the upkeep of horses and a list of Horse Patrol stations. There are several lists of patrolmen, giving name, age, height, place of birth, marital status and date of joining, for each individual. Many of these are extremely fragile and a modern transcription of some items is included in the file.

A service register of the **Bow Street Foot Patrol**, for 1821-1829, is to be found in MEPO 4/508. This register, which has no index, contains details of 174 officers, specifically name, place of residence, age and place of birth, height, marital status and number of children (if any), name of recommender, previous military service, date of appointment and date and reason for discharge, if appropriate. Drunkenness on duty seems to have been the downfall of more than one patrolman.

4.2.2 Metropolitan Police

Correspondence and papers, emanating from the Metropolitan Police Commissioner's office, relating to officers' pay and conditions and many other general police matters, are to be found in MEPO 1, MEPO 2, MEPO 3 and MEPO 4. Many of the pieces in MEPO 3 are closed for one hundred years because of the kinds of case they record, including rape, indecent exposure and baby farming. This class also offers some extraordinary insights into the crime of murder and official responses to it. For example, MEPO 3/787, which is a very large file of papers relating to a vacuum-cleaner salesman, Henry Seymour, executed at Oxford in 1931 for murdering Annie Kempson with a chisel, includes statements of evidence from persons acquainted with both murderer and victim, transcripts of part of the trial, official correspondence and telegrams, reports on other suspects, cuttings from the press, and discussion papers highlighting certain general principles brought out in the case. From the point of view of the history of the police, some of the most compelling items included in this file relate to the process of detection before Seymour became a suspect, such as following up clues about traders visiting the Kempson household in the weeks before the murder.

MEPO 6 contains printed registers of individuals either defined as **habitual criminals** under the Prevention of Crimes Act 1871 (i.e. having a previous conviction) or liberated from a sentence of penal servitude during the year (see fig.5). Arranged alphabetically by surname, each entry gives details of the individual's name and alias, date and place of birth, marital status, trade, appearance, date of discharge from prison, name of prison, length of sentence (NB - at least a month), and previous convictions. Family historians who lose track of an ancestor for whom there is some suspicion of a criminal record - perhaps he or she disappears unexpectedly in a census - might find it worth checking these registers which are very straightforward to use. Researchers into crime generally could find the level of detail available in this class valuable for statistical analysis and other purposes.

Case papers, petitions, photographs and offers of rewards, 1888-1894, relating to the **Whitechapel Murders of 1888**, better known as the crimes of 'Jack the Ripper', form MEPO 3/140 and MEPO 3/141. A detailed catalogue, arranged chronologically by victim, is available at the PRO; however, researchers should note that these records can be seen on microfilm only. A source sheet is available at the Reference Desk.

MEPO 20 consists of registers of murders and deaths by violence in the metropolitan area, including the deaths of women through abortion, 1891-1909, 1912-1917, and 1919-1966.

The work of officers of the Metropolitan Police in protecting members of the royal family is recorded in files such as that dealing with lodging allowance for officers on special duty, 1901-1902 (MEPO 2/572). Other aspects of the protection of the monarch are to be found in MEPO 2/44, a register of offences particularly against Queen Victoria and the Prince Consort by insane persons and vagrants, 1837-1852. This rather curious register notes each person's name and offence, with the names of witnesses and apprehender, and the result of the case. Some of the offences involved were clearly in the category of high treason: for example, the attempt by John Francis to shoot Queen Victoria in 1842, for which he was transported for life. Others fell into the category of trespass, such as that of Sarah Jones, a reputed prostitute, who was found asleep in the garden at Buckingham Palace and discharged on the order of Her Majesty. More difficult to categorize are those cases in which people were arrested for throwing a letter into the queen's carriage, annoying her at the opera, or wandering in the Mall whilst apparently insane.

There were a small number of assassination attempts against the queen's life in the 1840s and files relating to these are preserved in MEPO 3/18 and MEPO 3/19A and B. The case of Edward Oxford, who threatened Queen Victoria's life in June 1840, can be followed in MEPO 3/17. An eye-witness statement, by Edwin Burghart, describes the incident.

> ...[Burghart] was passing through the Green Park when he observed the Prisoner "Oxford" standing on Constitution Hill with his back to the rails shortly before the Queen's carriage came by, a Police Constable in uniform came by the Prisoner and told several persons to keep out of the way, when the carriage came opposite him "the Prisoner", he drew his right hand from under the flaps of his coat and appeared to take aim with a pistol and fired it off. He then took another pistol from his left hand into his right and fired again, some foreigners then ketched [sic] hold of the Prisoner and held him till a Constable came up...

The queen was unharmed. Police reports give details of Oxford's visitors whilst in detention, including some notes of conversations; and also indicate the procedures which were followed in investigating the background to the crime, for example, the searching of Oxford's lodgings.

As well as protecting the royal family, the Metropolitan Police have also been responsible for providing personal protection to visiting dignitaries: for example, during King Fuad of Egypt's visit to Great Britain in 1927 (MEPO 2/1914).

There are a number of classes which can be called upon for papers and photographs relating to individual officers and the work they undertook.

Researchers looking for details of particular officers may find what they want in various pieces in MEPO 4. The attestation ledgers, 1869-1958, which give the date of swearing-in (MEPO 4/352-360); joiners and leavers ledgers, 1829-1830 (MEPO 4/31-32); registers of leavers, 1889-1947 (MEPO 4/339-351); registers of deaths in service, 1829-1889 (MEPO 4/2); and other pieces, all provide the kind of information of considerable use to family historians looking for an ancestor in the Metropolitan Police.

Another set of records which might be of interest are the registers of **police pensioners**, 1852-1932, in MEPO 21. These are arranged by pension number, so in order to use them you need to have some idea of an individual's retirement date. Before 1923, these volumes give fairly full information, including the names of the officer's parents, next of kin, details of past promotions and his intended address on retirement. After 1923, the only extra information they tend to include, where appropriate, relates to the retiring officer's wife, noting the date of marriage and her place and date of birth, but sometimes even giving a brief description of her physical appearance.

Also of interest is MEPO 7, Commissioner's office papers relating to personnel matters such as promotion, transfers, awards and dismissal, 1829-1988, which is closed for fifty years; and MEPO 11, representative records, 1875-1976, emanating largely from one police unit, the West End Central Police Station, which are mainly closed for 75 years. There are also registers relating to decorations, honours and awards, 1909 to 1988, MEPO 22.

The records relating to the early history of the **women police constables' units** are not very extensive, but researchers looking at this aspect of police history will find much of value in MEPO 2, particularly MEPO 2/1748 and MEPO 2/1710, papers, 1916-1919, of the London Women Patrols Committee and, for the Second World War period, MEPO 2/6151-6170, which include records on recruitment, pay, allowances, training and other personnel matters. MEPO 2/7949 and MEPO 2/9436 include material relating to two important issues affecting the position of women in the police after the end of the war: whether married women should be permitted to remain in uniform and whether women should be recruited using the same examinations as men. It was agreed in the Police Council in June 1946 that the provisions excluding married women from the Metropolitan Police should be repealed (minutes dated 13 June 1946 in MEPO 2/7949).

For a study of the Metropolitan Police and its predecessors, the records which form the MEPO classes should be supplemented by a use of the many important papers to be found in Home Office classes. These include HO 61, Metropolitan Police Correspondence 1820-1840, including letters relating to appointments; and HO 58, which consists of quarterly accounts for police offices in the metropolis between 1813 and 1826, including details of salaries of named magistrates and clerks at work in the police courts, the costs of police officers, and fees received at each police office. They also provide a snapshot of petty offending in the London area. For example, among the accounts relating to the quarter ending on 31 March 1826 (HO 58/4) are references to a fine of ten shillings paid by a Francis Jackson for keeping an alehouse open during Divine Service on Sunday (3 January 1826), and a fine of five shillings paid by Henry Barrow on 13 February 1826 for drunkenness - a very common offence. Social historians may find these accounts of considerable interest, particularly for the juxtaposition of type of offence and level of fine, the easy identification of persistent petty offenders and the sporadic appearance of female miscreants. In general, they may be found to be quite revealing about the character of particular neighbourhoods.

Of similar use are the printed Daily Reports for 1828 to 1839 of the Metropolitan Police Offices held in HO 62, which include details of stolen property and persons brought before the magistrates, providing a further snapshot of the everyday offences being dealt with by the police force in its first decade, in this case often petty theft and common assault.

Copies of wide-ranging correspondence on police matters can be found in the Metropolitan Police Entry Books, 1899-1916, in HO 148, though the contemporary indexes to each volume are not very helpful. Items are arranged in each index in date order of despatch, within rough subject groupings; a typical entry, from HO 148/6 is: 'PC Lake sent to convalescent home - payment from Police Fund re, 20 Nov 1902, [page] 214.' The Police Entry Books Series II, 1887-1898, in HO 149, are similar in format, consisting of out-letters to the Commissioner of the Metropolitan Police relating to expenses, pensions and so on. These entry books, as with all examples of this kind of record, are likely to be of most interest to researchers investigating something very general (e.g. attitudes to police widows) for which simply browsing through the pages of each volume is likely to be productive.

Class HO 75 consists of *Hue and Cry* and *Police Gazette* 1828-1845, printed journals issued by Bow Street office. Other police publications are available in MEPO 6.

Researchers looking for pictorial evidence of policing will find MEPO 13, photographs and drawings, c.1770-1985, showing the development of the force, to be of value. The list of this class is arranged by subject. Plans and drawings of police stations and married officers' quarters, 1847-1957, are held as MEPO 9. For security reasons, these include only those buildings no longer in police use, in addition to those which have been demolished. Photographs of stations can be found in MEPO 14 (see fig.7) in two series: the first, the product of a special survey of station buildings undertaken between 1980 and 1983; and the second, older photographs extracted from other classes.

4.3 Policing the Provinces

Outside London, the establishment of local authority funded police forces was encouraged by the **County Police Act 1839**, a piece of permissive legislation which allowed JPs to set up paid county-wide police forces. Resistance to the establishment of such forces gradually diminished, partly as ratepayers came to realise that they were not a wholly new idea but built on existing police services and that they could provide a more cost-effective means of controlling crime and public disorder. Such was their acceptance by the mid-nineteenth century that the government was able to pass mandatory legislation, the **County and Borough Act 1856**, which required the establishment of a police force for any part of a county not yet covered, including boroughs. A similar Act was passed in 1857 which related to Scotland.

One result of this legislation was the proliferation of small forces which were relatively ineffective so, under the **Local Government Act 1888**, the situation was rationalized with the abolition of police forces run by boroughs with a population of less than 10,000. Further reorganization took place in 1946 following the **Police Act** of that year which abolished forty-five non-county police forces.

The records of police authorities outside the metropolis are not public records, and the survival of records of individual forces is patchy. Some remain with the originating body, whilst others have been deposited in local record offices.[5] There are relatively few records at the PRO which relate directly to the organization and operation of particular provincial police forces, though the Home Office series contains a considerable quantity of material which provides an overview of policing strategy nationally during most of the nineteenth and twentieth centuries. A number of classes consist of copies of letters sent by Home Office officials seeking information from police forces or commenting on particular situations. Equally, some Home Office classes contain many of the replies which were received and the documents which were compiled as a result of enquiries made of police forces and which can give a considerable insight into past government policy concerning the provision and role of police authorities. These include:

- HO 63, Annual Police Returns 1858-1869, relating to all police forces in England and Wales, including statistics;
- HO 66, Police Department, Register of Correspondence, 1856-1865;
- HO 150, Police Superannuation Entry Books, 1899-1917, out-letters relating to pensions;
- HO 158, Circulars, 1835-1984, issued to police and local authorities, arranged by date;
- HO 178, Edward Medal and King's Police Medal Out-letter Books, 1920-1921;
- HO 222, Police Department: Police Research Bulletin, 1967-1983, published by the Police Research and Planning Branch of the Home Office, for the information of police officers;
- HO 242, HM Inspectorate of Constabulary: Reports, Papers and Minutes, 1959-1974, including some plans and photographs dealing with the Great Train Robbery in 1963 and the proposed amalgamation of provincial police forces;
- HO 287, Police (POL Symbol Series) Files, 1949-1977, relating to Home Office functions and responsibilities in the field of police matters; and
- HO 358, Central Conference of Chief Constables: Minutes and Papers, 1918-1970, established in 1918 to promote co-ordination between police forces.

The police entry books for 1795-1921, in HO 65, include letters relating to various county, borough and Scottish police forces besides the Bow Street and other specific metropolitan police offices, and the Metropolitan Police in general to 1898. This class also includes an out-letter book for the

---

[5] See Ian Bridgeman and Clive Emsley, *A Guide to the Archives of the Police Forces of England and Wales* (Police History Society, 1989).

Birmingham Police Force, 1839-1842 (HO 65/10).

Files in HO 353 deal with the police's role in civil defence, 1947-1973, and are reflective of the Cold War fears of the period. One volume of printed memoranda issued centrally, and preserved as HO 347/3, relates to the county police forces in particular for the period 1839 to 1892. HO 45, as ever, merits investigation, with files on the origins of the detective force (HO 45/292), the strike of the Hull police for increased wages in 1853 (HO 45/4780), and all kinds of general police issues such as special allowances, the use of firearms, uniforms and pay.

Correspondence between the Treasury and the county and borough treasurers regarding police expenses, 1858-1872, will be found in T 15.

4.4   Policing Ireland (before 1922)

At the time of the Act of Union in 1800, the Irish police force was composed of a small number of poorly paid, part-time constables appointed by the local authorities, in this case the grand juries. It was not till the passage of the Irish (Constabulary (Ireland)) Act 1836 that a single unifed force was created, with the Lord Lieutenant of Ireland holding the powers of appointment, discharge and rule-making. The new Irish Constabulary (renamed the **Royal Irish Constabulary** in 1867) was responsible for keeping the peace in the whole of Ireland except Dublin, which maintained its own Metropolitan Police force.

Over time, the role of the Royal Irish Constabulary was extended from simple peace-keeping into such areas as the collection of statistics for government departments and the enforcement of regulations relating to explosives, food and drugs.

The Royal Irish Constabulary was disbanded in August 1922 and the service records of members of the force passed to the Home Office. HO 184, Irish Constabulary Records, 1816-1922, is the main source of information about individual officers, including details of name, age, religious affiliation and so on. HO 340, Royal Irish Constabulary (RIC Series) Files, 1920-1970, includes material relating to pensions and allowances, as does the Paymaster General's Office class PMG 48, Royal Irish Constabulary Pensions, etc, 1873-1925.

4.5 Investigations into Policing

In 1948 the Home Secretary appointed a special committee to consider police conditions of service including pay, under the chairmanship of Lord Oaksey. The transcripts of evidence which it received are in HO 298. A later investigatory body, the Royal Commission on the Police, established in 1960 and chaired by Sir Henry Urmston Willink, was asked to make recommendations on the constitution and functions of local police forces, the status and accountability of individual officers, dealing with complaints against the police and the way in which police pay should be determined. Its records, forming HO 272, consist of minutes and papers which provide much evidence on the state of the provincial police forces in the period after the Second World War. Some of the pieces are closed for seventy-five years.

The records of two later investigations into aspects of policing are also preserved at the PRO. The first, the Committee of Inquiry on the Police, especially concerning the role of staff associations, has records for 1977-1979 in BS 17. A further investigation was carried out by the Committee of Inquiry into the Payment and Conditions of the Non-Home Department Police Forces, 1978. Most of this committee's records, in class BA 4, are closed till 2009, but a few pieces of evidence submitted by individual forces, such as the Belfast Harbour Police, and the final report published in 1979 (BA 4/34), are already accessible.

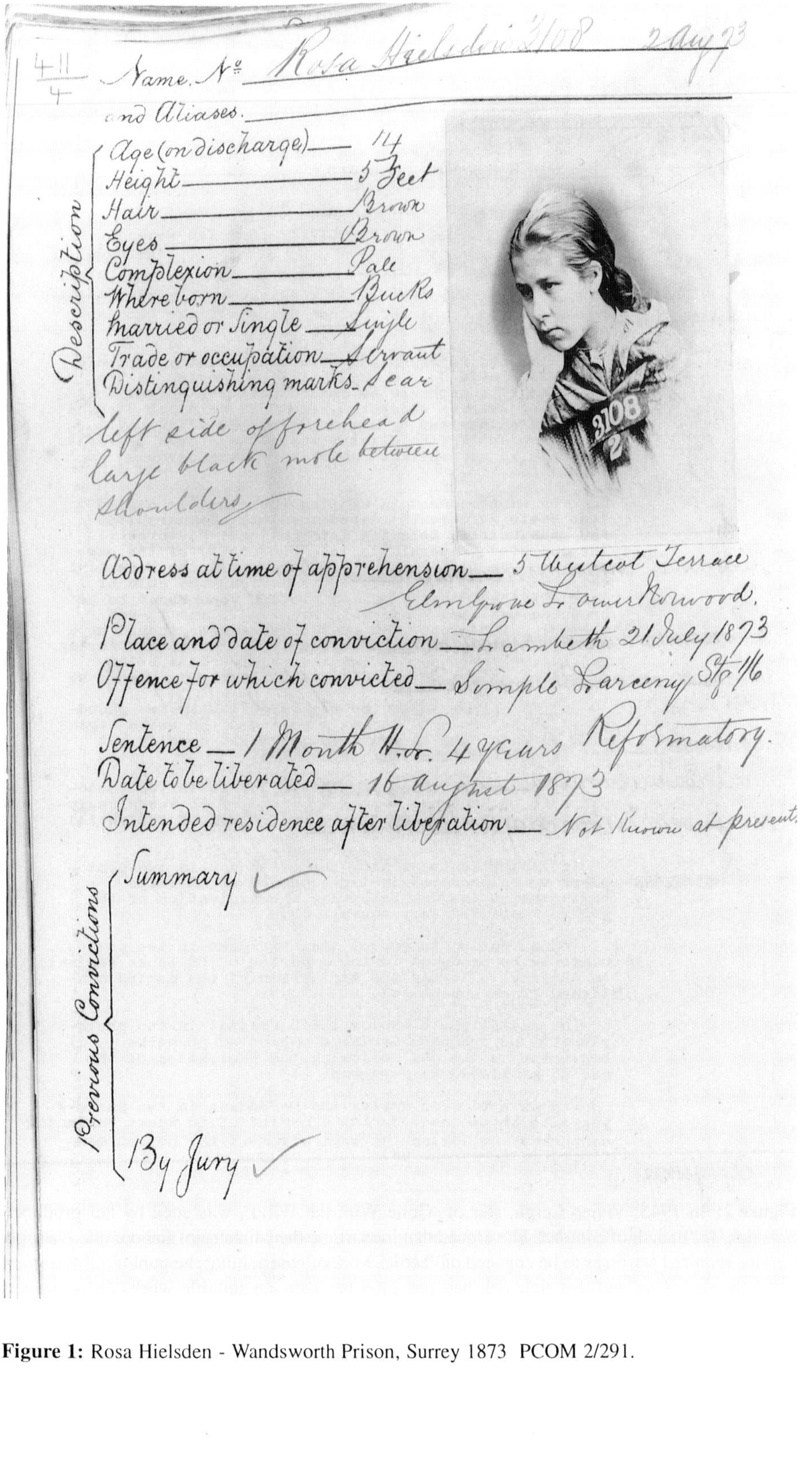

4 11
—
4

Name. Nº   _Rosa Hielsden 3108   2 Aug 73_

and Aliases.

Description

Age (on discharge)——— 14
Height———————— 5 Feet
Hair——————————— Brown
Eyes——————————— Brown
Complexion————————— Pale
Where born————————— Bucks
Married or Single————— Single
Trade or occupation——— Servant
Distinguishing marks— Scar
left side of forehead
large black mole between
shoulders

Address at time of apprehension— 5 Wyteot Terrace
Elmgrove Lower Norwood.
Place and date of conviction— Lambeth 21 July 1873
Offence for which convicted— Simple Larceny Stg 1/6

Sentence— 1 Month H. or. 4 years Reformatory.
Date to be liberated— 16 August 1873
Intended residence after liberation— Not Known at present.

Previous Convictions

Summary ✓

By Jury ✓

Figure 1: Rosa Hielsden - Wandsworth Prison, Surrey 1873 PCOM 2/291.

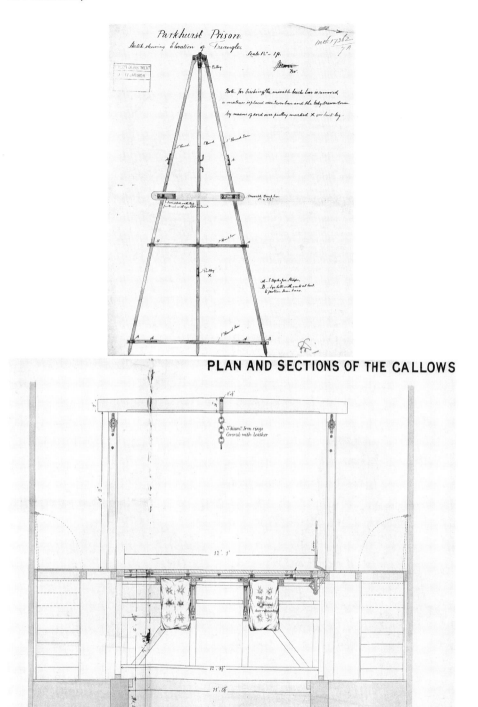

Figure 12: Birching triangle for use at Parkhurst Prison, 1846   PCOM 7/386/17262/70.

Figure 13: Newgate Gaol – Gallows, 1881   HO 144/18/46327.

Police Office, Great Marlborough Street.

AN ACCOUNT of all PENALTIES and FORFEITURES, and Shares thereof, received at the said Office, in the Quarter ending the 31st Day of March 1825

1825	NAME OF PARTY.	OFFENCE.	L.	S.	D.
Jany 1st	John Child having lead in his possession he could not account for		1	—	—
3d	Lester Bollerson	Drunkenness	—	5	—
4	Joseph Hill	Interrupting free passage	1	"	"
5	John Moody	The like	1	"	"
6	Margt Hawden, Wm Bruce, Jas Summers & Jos. Sullivan	The like 20 each	4	"	"
	Margt McHew & 3 others	Drunkenness 5 each	1	"	"
7	Benj. Burn, a Victualler	keeping open late hours	5	"	"
	Jn Brookbanks, Jn Stokes & Wm Walker	Exercising their worldly labour on the Lords Day 3/4 each	—	10	"
14	Thos Hawkins, Jos. Dalton & Jn Jones	The like 3/4 each	"	10	"
	John Holland	Drunkenness	"	5	"
15	Jn Madden & Robt Shankes	The like 5 each	"	10	"
	Wm Rudd, a Victualler, suffering	tipling during Divine Service	"	15	"
	Jacob Ainns	The like	"	5	"
17	Jn Sanders, Dennis Murray & Jn Dwyer	Drunkenness 5 each	"	15	"
18	Jn Williams, Robt Moorhead, Robt Dixon, Jas Taylor, Rd Crump & Jn Coombe	The like 5 each	1	10	"
19	Wm Hudson	The like	"	5	"
20	Geo Martin, Jos. Atherton & Jos. Philpot	Interrupting free passage 20 each	3	"	"
21	David Jones, Wm Dobbins, Nat Warren & W Hales	Exercising their worldly labour on the Lords Day 3/4 each		13	4
22	Jas McGorvan, Wm Hardstaff, Sam Watson, Geo Woodhouse & G Bavenstock	Victuallers for suffering tipling at late hours 5 each	1	10	"
	Wm Mullins, Wm Crouch & Danl Clear	Exercising their worldly labour on the Lords Day 3/4 each	"	10	"
24	Joseph Bubb	Obstructing a Watchman	"	5	"
	Thos Williams, Geo Williams, Jn Ormsby & Wm Platt	Drunkenness 5 each	1	"	"
25	F. W. Raulback & Jn White	victuallers keeping open late hours 20 each	2	"	"
26	Vincent Penny, J. Hailey, Geo Whitecomb, Mich Hogan & Ann Jones	Drunkenness 5 each	1	5	0
	Wm Mathews exercising worldly labour on the Lords Day		"	3	4
		Carried forward - -	28	16	8

Figure 14: Fines levied at Great Marlborough Street Police Office, in 1825   HO 58/4.

Figure 15: Pupils from Paisley Industrial School at Summer Camp, Millport 1914   MH 102/2692.

Chapter 5: AT THE TRIAL'S END

5.1 Sentencing

The sentencing of those found guilty of a criminal offence is a function of the judiciary, using their discretion to determine a just punishment within the boundaries set down by statute and common law. In deciding upon a sentence, judges should take into account aggravating or mitigating circumstances, and the sentence given may be less severe for those who pleaded guilty at an early stage or who helped in the prosecution of others. There are very few offences for which the law as it presently stands prescribes specific punishments. The most important is murder, for which there is a mandatory sentence of life imprisonment.

In the wake of the reduction of offences earning capital punishment in the early nineteenth century, the range of penalties available to the courts had been somewhat enlarged, but the development had taken place in a haphazard and not entirely consistent way. It was, in particular, felt that the statute law and the common law were sometimes unhelpfully at odds with one another. There was also growing criticism of the arbitrariness of sentencing, which meant that similar offences could gain vastly differing sentences, even at the same sitting of a court.

In 1833 eight members of a Criminal Law Commission were appointed by the home secretary to investigate all the statutes and common law touching on crime and punishment, with a view to combining them into a single body of criminal law. The Criminal Law Commissioners sought to link crimes and punishments to enhance their deterrent effect. In their first report, they proposed the introduction of four classes of crime and punishment: very serious, earning death; serious, earning transportation for life or ten years imprisonment; middling, earning less than ten years imprisonment; and petty, to be punished with a fine or transportation for seven years. Unfortunately, this apparent clarity and simplicity soon came to elude the Commissioners who, by their seventh report, were suggesting forty-five classes.

A new Commission for Revising and Consolidating the Criminal Law was appointed in 1845. In its report, it reduced the forty-five classes to eighteen, restoring a large degree of judicial discretion, particularly regarding aggravating circumstances. From 1848, attempts were made to have this criminal code entered into law. However, codification faced a great deal of opposition. Critics argued that the proposal was unworkable: it would be in conflict with the traditions of England's legal and political traditions, besides which it would be dangerously inflexible and would need constant alteration in order to keep up with trends and developments in crime and punishment. The judiciary, in particular, were hostile to the effective abolition of the common law which codification would entail. No changes to the law of any great significance came about as a result of the work of these two Commissions.

A Commission to Consider and Consolidate the Statute Law was appointed in 1854. It succeeded in bringing about a number of small changes to the sentencing structure, most importantly the abolition of the death penalty for attempted murder in 1861. However, it did not suggest the introduction of a code. Further attempts to bring about codification in the 1870s failed.

In the 1880s, the home secretary initiated a debate between himself, the lord chancellor and the judiciary on the subject of sentencing. He suggested that greater leniency in sentencing would be appropriate given the declining crime rate and urged that judges should take greater care to match the sentence given to the circumstances of the individual offender.

This attempt at interference in the judicial process was firmly rebuffed, as were efforts to establish a Royal Commission to investigate ways of promoting uniformity in sentencing. There have been later attempts to influence sentencing practice, including the Criminal Justice Act 1991 which introduced unit fines to the magistrates' courts, but all have proved unsuccessful.

The Court of Criminal Appeal, which was established in 1907, was used initially only to review sentences on appeal. It tended to take a conservative line, reducing few sentences; however, its work gradually set new lower benchmarks for certain punishments and promoted the view that the maximum penalty should be reserved for the worst examples of a crime. The Court of Criminal Appeal was essentially a Home Office undertaking, and records relating to its operation may be found in HO classes (for example, HO 45/10337/139064). The court's registers are in J 81 and some cases files, mainly from 1956, are in J 82. No pre-1945 files have survived. Some files are closed for 75 years.

It does, however, require some ingenuity to find records at the PRO which deal with the issue of sentencing. Given the history outlined above, there is surprisingly little surviving discussion of the questions which were raised by proposals for standardization and codification. A few papers can be found among the records of the Lord Chancellor's Department, particularly in LCO 1 and LCO 2.

As with so many other issues, it is a close examination of classes HO 45 and HO 144 which is likely to bear the most fruit. For example, HO 144/943/A60866 consists of notes on the exercise of the prerogative of mercy and the standardization of sentences, 1899-1912, while consistently light sentences passed by judges in Liverpool and Salford are discussed critically in HO 45/9710/A51112 and HO 144/1087/194175 respectively.

Papers relating to individual cases may also shed some light on sentencing practices prevailing at the time of conviction. A very full and interesting example is the file held as HO 291/63, which concerns the case of six members of the Campaign for Nuclear Disarmament who were imprisoned in 1962 for various terms for conspiring to commit a breach of the Official Secrets Act 1911. A number of MPs appealed to the Home Secretary to invoke the prerogative of mercy, but he refused on the grounds that this would lend credence to statements that the six were political prisoners.

The records of quarter and petty sessions, which are held by local record offices, should also be of general interest, not least for statistical analysis of sentencing practice.

5.2 Criminal Insanity

5.2.1 Insanity as a Defence

Before 1843, about a tenth of persons accused of a crime were declared unfit to plead or acquitted as insane. By 1908-1913, this had risen to a third. This rise was partly due to the formulation of a reasonably precise rule under which the defence of insanity could be offered: the **M'Naghten Rule.**

This was named after Daniel M'Naghten who shot and killed Sir Robert Peel's secretary, Drummond, believing him to be Peel. M'Naghten was

Hospital, the institution designed to hold the criminally insane, which had been opened in 1863 as an asylum for criminal lunatics under the Criminal Lunatic Asylum Act 1860. Until 1948 the administration of Broadmoor Hospital was in the remit of the Home Office. In that year the Criminal Justice Act passed responsibility to the Board of Control. This transfer had taken some time to negotiate and had posed numerous problems. For instance, memoranda and correspondence, 1937-1941, in MH 51/840, indicate that because the Home Office lacked medical expertise, the supervision of Broadmoor had been left in the hands of an unqualified council of local worthies which had, according to a Ministry of Health memorandum of February 1939, 'failed altogether to keep abreast of the advances that are constantly being made in the treatment of mental patients.' This Council of Supervision required careful handling and the local political situation was clearly very sensitive. Following the dissolution of the Board of Control in 1960 as a result of the Mental Health Act 1959, Broadmoor and the nation's other special hospitals came under the direct management of the Ministry of Health.

As a result of the shared responsibilities between departments for identifying and dealing with the criminally insane, relevant papers are scattered throughout the records of the Home Office, Lord Chancellor's Department and the various bodies and departments responsible for health. Files of some importance are particularly to be found in the following classes.

5.2.3 Home Office Records

HO 119/5 includes a small number of papers on the Metropolitan Lunacy Commission, 1829-1830. Some correspondence relates to the revocation in 1829, under 9 George IV, c 41, of licences granted to lunatic asylums in Plaistow and Edmonton. A report on the Plaistow asylum highlighted the promiscuous mingling of male and female patients that was permitted and noted that the patients were dirty, untreated, and left without religious instruction. In addition, this piece includes a note of the superintendent's verbal evidence given in his defence before the Commission. From the same year comes a long and detailed report on the condition of asylums in and around London, addressed to Robert Peel. While not strictly related to criminal lunacy, these papers show some of the problems that were presented to government authorities by early mental hospitals.

HO 44, Home Office: Domestic Correspondence, 1820-1861, includes other papers relating to the Metropolitan Lunacy Commission. HO 347/4 includes some miscellaneous printed memoranda relating to prisons and Broadmoor Hospital.

HO 145 consists of Home Office: Criminal Lunacy Warrant and Entry Books, 1882-1921. All the volumes follow a similar format. Copies of Home Office out-letters refer to individual cases and include: replies to appeals by relatives for release from Broadmoor; warrants for the transfer of certified prisoners from prisons to asylums; requests for information on the progress or background of cases; and transfers of individuals between various institutions. HO 145/17, to take one volume as an example, covers the period October 1907 to September 1908. It includes: warrants under the Criminal Lunatic Asylums Act 1860 (23 & 24 Victoria, c 75, s 2) for removal of prisoners to Broadmoor, giving details of the offence committed and the sentence of the court; letters relating to the appointment and promotion of staff at Broadmoor, both male and female (see, for example, a letter agreeing to the promotion of three male staff, dated 4 February 1908, on p 339); copies of warrants granting a conditional discharge; and letters to relatives being permitted to take charge of former inmates (see, for example, p 367). This volume would be of almost no use to family historians, as it is arranged in date order and to browse through the pages looking for occasional mentions of particular names would be time-consuming and probably fruitless. However, it could be used to throw considerable light on the relationship between the Home Office and Broadmoor (and also other institutions); while the various warrants offer material for analysis relating to offences, sentences, geographical incidence of certification, and the policies of the courts involved.

One class which is likely to be of interest to future researchers into the definition of and response to criminal insanity is HO 343, Home Office: Mental Patients (MNP Series) Files, 1927-1986. This class, consisting of forty-three pieces, includes personal material relating to individual Broadmoor patients, but is for the present entirely closed.

A fascinating volume relating to both male and female criminal lunatics held in **Bethlem Hospital**, 1823-1835, forms part of HO 20/13 (see fig.8). This volume appears to be a fair copy of the Bethlem Hospital admissions register, including copies of certification statements, and giving details of name, age, sex, crime, when and where arraigned on trial with the verdict, parish or origin, previous character and conduct, date of removal to Bethlem, and date of discharge. Many of the entries incorporate remarks on the behaviour of the individual concerned before trial or whilst an inmate of the institution.

At the back of this volume there is a list of other persons found guilty of a crime but insane between 1804 and 1839, with a note of their crimes and the asylum to which they were each removed. Though this register lacks any kind of names index, it could be of interest to genealogists. In a wider context, it is revealing of how mental disorder was defined and described in this period, demonstrating some of the kinds of behaviour that might be interpreted as insane.

Finally, with respect to the Home Office's responsibilities in this area, the classes HO 45 and HO 144 will, as always, merit investigation.

5.2.4 Board of Control / Health Departments' Records

The Board of Control: Registers of Admission of Patients, 1846-1960, in MH 94, give details of the legal and medical circumstances surrounding the admission of individuals into mental asylums. They include occasional references to patients received at Broadmoor Hospital. The registers provide information on the name, sex, date of admission, name of asylum, date of discharge or death, with cause of death if applicable, and a statement as to whether the patient had recovered, relapsed or failed to improve at all. The volumes are in chronological order (MH 94/19 covers, for example, admissions between June 1864 and December 1866) and the entries within each are grouped together by the first letter of the surname. These volumes are potentially of interest to researchers looking into their family history if they suspect that an ancestor may, at some point, have entered an asylum, whether as a criminal lunatic or for other reasons.

Case files for patients in Broadmoor and Rampton are contained in MH 103, DHSS: Special Hospitals, Patients' Files, 1913-1981. The whole class, consisting of 309 files, is closed for seventy-five years.

MH 118 is arguably the most important class available for information on the practical management of criminal lunacy in the twentieth century consisting, as it does, of the Board of Control's Special Hospitals' Registered Files. It includes files on: staff appointments, salary and discipline; dietaries; inspection; medical treatment; security; education; and so on, covering all the many aspects of running a secure residential institution. MH 118/2, for example, is a bundle of papers, 1917-1955, relating to the diet offered to both staff and patients, the abolition of the beer allowance for staff and its replacement by a salary increase, and the merits of the dietary compared with the food controller's limits in 1917.

MH 121 consists of the records of the Royal Commission on the Law relating to Mental Illness and Mental Deficiency, 1952-1957, which was chaired by Lord Percy of Newcastle and the report of which brought about the Mental Health Act 1959. Its royal warrant specifically excluded consideration of the position of Broadmoor patients, though the Commission's final report did include a few comments and reminded readers that many of its conclusions could be applied to the 'special hospitals'. A file of correspondence, dated 1955, relating to Rampton Criminal Lunatic Asylum, Retford, exists as MH 121/34, but is closed for seventy-five years. MH 121/6 includes a draft of the proposed Royal Warrant for appointing the Commission, together with correspondence on the establishment of the Commission's office facilities and engagement of administrative staff, with extracts from Hansard, accounts and estimates of likely expenditure. This piece provides a well-documented example of the office, or 'backstage', side of a temporary Commission.

Class MH 140, Ministry of Health: Mental Health Act 1959, General Files, 1958-1966, includes papers of the Special Hospitals Working Party as MH 140/58-73. Some of these pieces are closed for seventy-five years. A particularly interesting file, MH 140/58, shows the political manoeuvring that can form the background to the creation of such a body and throws some light on the Civil Service culture of the period. Correspondence of officials found in this file is suggestive of rivalry between the Home Office and the various health authorities, especially, from the Board of Control's view point, over the need to allow the Home Office to be involved without permitting them the scope to be obstructive. Much concern was also being shown by officials that the Special Hospitals Working Party should be seen to be a well-balanced body, rather than looking, as one memo puts it, 'too much like the Board of Control plus a few doctors brought in from outside.'

Specimens of forms relating to Broadmoor Hospital are held in MH 900/14. These consist of forms for the committal and transfer of patients, for the recording of interviews between staff and relatives of patients, and for noting personal or medical information about individuals, such as their mental state and physical health. Included is a copy of the printed booklet *Broadmoor Institution: Instructions for the Guidance of Nursing and Other Staff,* which was issued to staff and summarized their duties and responsibilities in their relationship with patients.

Other classes of possible interest are: MH 50, Lunacy Commission and Board of Control: minutes, 1845-1960, in which there are occasional, brief mentions of Broadmoor; MH 51, Lunacy Commission and Board of Control: Correspondence and Papers, 1798-1971; and MH 53, Public Health and Poor Law Series: Local Government Administration, General Files, 1910-1972, particularly MH 53/54, which is evidence presented to the Minister of Health by the Metropolitan Asylum Board in 1927.

5.2.5 Miscellaneous Records

MEPO 3, Metropolitan Police: Office of the Commissioner, Correspondence and Papers - Special Series, 1830-1974, includes papers on the working of the lunacy laws, such as MEPO 3/2424 on the possible treatment of attempted suicides as insane and MEPO 3/2516 on the correct procedures to be followed when dealing with persons of unsound mind, 1938-1947 (closed for seventy-five years).

A Works Department class, WORK 38, includes plans of Broadmoor Criminal Lunatic Asylum's chapel, gallery, day room, deputy superintendent's house and centre building (WORK 38/332-342).

The 'unregistered papers' of the Lord Chancellor's Department in LCO 1 may also be found to be of some limited use.

Chapter 6 PUNISHMENTS

6.1 Capital Punishment

Before the Restoration, there were comparatively few offences for which death was the prescribed sentence. Felonies, such as murder, arson, rape or robbery, would earn the death penalty, whilst those convicted of misdemeanours, such as petty thefts and assaults, would be sentenced to a lesser form of punishment like whipping or the pillory.

The early eighteenth century saw the beginning of a rapid growth in the number of capital crimes with the passing into law of a large number of penal measures, many promoted by pressure groups and wealthy individuals. The most infamous of these pieces of legislation was the Criminal Law Act 1722, commonly known as the Waltham Black Act (9 George I, c 22) which criminalized many previously legal activities, such as taking fruit from trees, and made them punishable by death. The Black Act generally reflected an increasing commercialization of landed estates and was intended to protect the newly developing property rights of estate holders against small farmers and tenants who wished to exercize traditional rights on common and waste lands.

Other economic developments in the eighteenth century were also reflected in increasingly harsh legislation, particularly aimed against forgery and counterfeiting, which had become more of a problem through the evolution of a system of banking based on the exchange of paper notes. The laws against forgery were among the most rigorously enforced in the eighteenth century, with approximately two-thirds of those convicted actually executed.[1] Still further legislation dealt with the threats to business posed by discontented workers fearing unemployment through the application of new technology. As a result of the many legislative changes, well over two hundred crimes were punishable by death at the time of the Napoleonic Wars. Although many were hanged for murder, most of those hanged during the eighteenth century had committed offences against property.

Two of the nineteenth century home secretaries, Sir Samuel Romilly and Sir Robert Peel, inspired by both humanitarianism and a desire for

---

[1] Michael Ignatieff, *A just measure of pain: The penitentiary in the Industrial Revolution, 1750-1850* (Penguin, 1978), p 17

governmental efficiency, sought to reduce and rationalize the law as it touched on capital punishment. Romilly's first act in this connection, in the face of considerable opposition, was to abolish the death penalty in 1808 for the crime of picking pockets of goods of the value of twelvepence. Almost all of Romilly's later attempts to bring reform failed, but Peel was more successful. By 1832, housebreaking, sheep stealing and forgery were no longer capital offences and, after 1838, executions were largely limited to those convicted of murder.

It is, however, worth mentioning that despite the increase in the number of crimes earning the sentence of death in the eighteenth century, there had been no corresponding increase in the number of executions. Historians have proposed various reasons for this.

Firstly, it has been suggested that juries were unwilling to convict individuals of thefts which were punishable by death, feeling the punishment to be out of proportion to the crime. It is suggested that they committed 'pious perjury' by undervaluing stolen items where the value of goods stolen turned the offence from a misdemeanour, punishable by transportation, to a capital felony. A jury might also reduce a charge by finding only part of it to be true, eg highway robbery was capital only if the victim was put in fear: no fear, no hanging.

Secondly, in some instances, the convicted could claim benefit of clergy, an ancient but, by the eighteenth century, thoroughly bastardized right, which allowed anyone able to read (or recite from memory) a specified psalm to escape execution.

Thirdly, historians have blamed poor rates of detection and the system of private prosecution for allowing criminals to slip through the legal net altogether,[2] although an examination of the clear up rates by to-day's police forces hardly point to much change in that respect.

---

[2]. See for example, Christopher Harding et al, *Imprisonment in England and Wales: A concise history* (Croom Helm, 1985), pp 58-59.

6.1.1 Pardons

Another important factor in keeping down the number of executions was the increasing availability of alternatives, such as transportation and imprisonment, which facilitated the use of the royal prerogative from the early eighteenth century and allowed death sentences to be commuted accordingly. The royal prerogative was exercized, after 1782, through the home secretary who would make his decision taking into account factors such as: the youth or agedness of the convicted person; any evidence of insanity or mental disease; the degree of provocation involved in the crime (a defence which tended to be applied most successfully by men convicted of killing a drunken or unfaithful wife); the opinion of the judge and jury and whether they had recommended mercy; and the existence of any doubt over guilt.

Conditional pardons, as they were known, were most commonly granted for newer capital offences and in cases of infanticide. The last execution of a woman for this crime took place in 1849. **Free pardons**, signifying that a conviction was to be completely disregarded, as if it had never been, would be granted to individuals for whom convincing evidence of innocence could be produced. Earlier, they were used for the guilty, too, and remain, technically, an exercize of mercy not a statement of innocence. Though there was some inevitable arbitrariness in the application of the royal prerogative, it was quite generously applied so that, for example, between 1866 and 1881 almost half those sentenced to death were reprieved. Forty per cent of those committed for trial for a capital offence were acquitted and around twenty per cent found guilty but insane. Therefore only around twenty per cent of those accused of a capital crime between these years were actually executed.[3]

Registers of remissions and pardons, 1887 to 1960, are preserved in HO 188. A **remission** was an act of clemency, usually awarded to a convicted person who had offered substantive assistance to the authorities, which removed some of the consequences of the conviction, by, for example, shortening the period of imprisonment which had to be served. Each volume has an index of sorts, with the convicted persons grouped together by the first initial of their surnames. The cases are described in some detail with reasons given for mercy being shown. Women feature prominently, both

---

[3] Radzinowicz and Hood, pp 678-679

as murder victims - particularly at the hands of their husbands or lovers - and as the perpetrators of infanticide. Abortion cases are also common. Two typical examples are the cases of Sarah Ann Eden and Franz Ludwig Hulstrom which are described in HO 188/3.

In the autumn of 1895, Sarah Ann Eden:

> was convicted of murder, she having been instrumental in causing the death of a married woman whom she had attended as nurse in former confinements, by the performance upon her, at the patient's solicitation, of an illegal operation [i.e. an abortion].
>
> No woman has, according to the Home Office records for the past 50 years, been executed for such a crime, and the Secretary of State has accordingly advised the respite of the Capital Sentence with a view to commutation to Penal Servitude for Life.

The husband of the dead woman was also convicted of murder, condemned and reprieved to serve a life sentence.

Franz Ludwig Hulstrom was a lodging-house keeper, convicted at Cardiff Assizes of shooting his wife. The register notes that he was

> reported to have been of good behaviour and quiet disposition, whereas his wife's intemperate habits were believed to have led to the death of four of their children. She came home drunk on the night of the murder. Immediately afterwards, in a fit of violent passion, the prisoner fired the fatal shot with a revolver which he had in his possession.
>
> The jury found that he had acted under great provocation and the learned judge considered the case was not one for the extreme penalty of the law and it is accordingly proposed to commute the death sentence to one of Penal Servitude for Life.

Hulstrom was duly reprieved.

Original appeals (or petitions) for mercy made by convicted persons between

1821 and 1839 can be found in HO 17. These are arranged in bundles by coded alphabetical references and are indexed, by the surname of the petitioner, in HO 19. It should be noted that the alphabetical reference bears no relationship to the surname. For example, the petition coded Cp 50 relates to a John Gorman convicted of highway robbery in 1830. His petition is accompanied by a sad appeal from his wife for mercy for the sake of their two small children and a statement of forgiveness from the person whom Gorman robbed, but this was to no avail. The petition is marked 'Law to take its course' and Gorman was presumably executed. The registers in HO 19 do not contain any details of the offences for which petitioners had been convicted. For this information you need to go to the actual petitions in HO 17.

Other bundles of papers relating to appeals for mercy are to be found in HO 6, i.e. letters and statements written by circuit judges between 1816 and 1840 which include recommendations of mercy in certain cases in which they had been obliged to give a sentence of death. These missives were addressed to the monarch in a formal manner, describing the convicted persons and the circumstances surrounding the crime which led the judges to believe clemency was justified. The alternative punishment which they usually suggested was transportation for life. The recommendation for mercy was not always heeded. Related material may also be found among the Home Office's Domestic Correspondence, 1782-1820, in HO 42.

6.1.2 Executions and Executioners

The criminal cases entry books for 1899 to 1921, in HO 163, include some Home Office out-letters discussing condemned persons, usually replying in the negative to correspondents making appeals for mercy. MEPO 3, a class which includes a great many pieces dealing with cases of murder, also contains some papers relating to executions: for example, MEPO 3/790, papers relating to the execution of Frederick William Parker and Albert Probert for the murder of Joseph Bedford at Portslade, 1933-1934.

A number of Home Office and Prison Commission classes incorporate material relating to individual condemned prisoners. A general source is the criminal registers for England and Wales for 1805 to 1892 in HO 27, which give details of trial results, sentences and the date of execution, if appropriate, and often include some personal details. These are useful for tracing persons convicted of both capital and non-capital offences.

The complete records of nine condemned prisoners have been kept in HO 336 as an example of the kinds of material generated by the legal and prison authorities following a person's conviction of a capital offence. These records would have been kept at the prison where the convict was interred and moved with him if he was transferred. PCOM 8 also contains records of prisoners convicted of capital crimes, but are all subject to one hundred years closure, and some non-capital cases, such as the Suffragette leader, Emmeline Pankhurst (see fig.9).

Further personal files can be found in PCOM 9/2026-2096, most of which are available for consultation. These include a file (PCOM 9/2084) on Ruth Ellis, the last woman to be executed in England, hanged in 1955 for murder. It contains medical information, copies of letters written by her when in prison, newspaper cuttings, assessments of her mental state and notes on her visitors, as well as the official statement recording her execution (see fig.10). Obviously the Ellis file is not quite typical, but it is fair to say that these kinds of papers are both moving and revealing of the way in which the condemned were perceived by their guardians and the public.

Until 1868, when the Capital Punishment Amendment Act was passed, executions in England were public events (see fig.11). In the metropolis, till 1783, executions took place roughly every six weeks at Tyburn (near where Marble Arch now stands). The convicted prisoners were transported to Tyburn through some of the city's most busy streets in a ritualized public procession from Newgate gaol at the Old Bailey. After 1783, executions took place just outside Newgate's walls, the reason for the change being the irreverent and sometimes dangerous conduct of the crowds which gathered along the route to and at the Tyburn gallows to witness executions. PCOM 2/190 is a register of the prisoners under sentence of death received at Newgate Gaol between 1817 and 1837. There is no index and the handwriting is difficult to read, but it is worth persevering especially for the information on women under sentence of death between 1817 and 1834.

In the provinces, the gallows were erected in front of town halls, in market squares, or in other prominent thoroughfares where the maximum publicity could be guaranteed. Just as in London, an inappropriately festive atmosphere amongst the spectators often went with a hanging. However, public executions sometimes had more serious consequences for on-lookers.

Papers in HO 45/681 describe the terrible tragedy which accompanied the execution in Nottingham in the summer of 1844 of William Saville for the murder of his wife and children. The case had become notorious in the locality and, on the day of the execution, a great crowd gathered to watch it take place. Afterwards, the pressure of the crowd was so great in the narrow streets that panic set in and twelve people, mostly women and children, were trampled to death with sixteen others injured. Within days some of the town's magistrates were petitioning the home secretary to permit them to relocate the place of execution away from the County Hall, in the cramped town centre, to a place nearer the prison. Others wrote to voice their objections to change. The home secretary in reply gave a clear statement of the reasons why he and many others felt that executions had to be public events. 'The principal object of capital punishment,' he wrote,

> is the terror of the Example; and no place can be considered fit for this purpose, where a large multitude of spectators may not assemble in safety sufficiently near to the scaffold to recognize the person of the criminal; and some of the Bye Standers should be able to hear any words of warning he may address to them. (HO 45/681, memorandum 24 August 1844)

The home secretary sided with those objecting to change and that, for the time being, was that.

On the practical aspects of execution, researchers will find PCOM 8, one of the main classes for Prison Commission registered papers, of considerable interest. For example, material on the tolling of the prison bell and hoisting of the black flag signifying an execution can be found in PCOM 8/210. PCOM 8/199-207 include papers considering the general treatment of prisoners awaiting execution, such as the permissibility of smoking, the frequency with which letters could be sent or received and the number of visitors who might be received.

Not all the available documents dealing with the death penalty are as palatable as these. For example, PCOM 8/212, which is innocuously titled 'Table of drops 1902-04' in the class list, contains some gruesome details of bungled executions amongst the discussion of whether executioners were ignoring the specified table of drops to be used in a hanging. Excessively long or short drops had resulted in a number of decapitations; and other unpleasant instances had arisen when a miscalculation on the executioner's part had led to throat wounds from a suicide attempt being reopened, death taking up to five minutes and horrible convulsions of the condemned person's body whilst hanging. HO 144/18/46327 includes a plan of the gallows at Newgate Prison in 1881 (see fig.13).

A substantial proportion of the Home Office and Prison Commission files dealing with capital punishment are devoted to the issue of choosing, disciplining and paying the executioner. Traditionally, the process by which executioners were selected had been relatively informal, with the ultimate decision in each case resting with the high sheriff of any given county. However, the officials of the Home Office became convinced that some central intervention was needed when the reputed poor conduct and undeniably shoddy work of James Berry, the chief executioner of the 1880s, came to their attention. Not only was it rumoured that he was a drunkard: worse, it was said that he was selling pieces of rope to members of the public as souvenirs of more celebrated hangings (HO 144/18/46327). Berry was also responsible for a number of shocking incidents during executions, especially decapitations.

To overcome the dependence of local sheriffs on the limited number of executioners existing, some of whom were clearly incompetent, the Home Office put in place a formal selection and training system for hangmen and their assistants. Some of the papers of a special committee, appointed by the home secretary in January 1890 to interview prospective executioners, are preserved in HO 144/212/A48697D. They interviewed and approved six men: James Billington, a barber by trade; Francis Gardner, a gamekeeper; Robert Wade, a saddler; James Stanhope, an insurance agent; John Thompson, a wheelwright; and John Ecles, a former police constable. Of these, Billington and Thompson had previous experience in the job. Billington came, in fact, from a Bolton family which provided three executioners over a thirty year period. A file on William Billington, who was dismissed from his post in 1903 following a conviction for neglecting his family, forms PCOM 8/193.

There was actually some discussion among prison officials and politicians on the merits of selecting candidates expressly because they could provide youthful male relatives to act as assistant executioners (PCOM 8/189), but this does not really seem to have swayed interviewing committee members in their choices.

Executioners seem to have been held in generally low regard by the officials and policitians who had dealings with them. Prison governors sometimes criticized them for their sloppy work and low intelligence (see, for example, comments about James Billington in PCOM 8/212); while officials at the Home Office felt no compunction about totally ignoring executioners' letters and requests, having the local police keep them under surveillance, and threatening them with dire consequences if they dared to break any of the rules under which they held their positions (for example, by speaking to the press). Indeed, the executioner seems to have looked upon as little better than the murderers he was employed to hang. Some correspondents went so far as to suggest that executioners should not be permitted to live in a small town or village because of the infamy their presence visited upon the community. An awareness of these kinds of prejudice may have been behind the actions of the wife of William Billington who wrote to the Home Office anonymously, accusing him of gross drunkenness in an unsuccessful effort to have him excluded from the position of executioner (PCOM 8/193, letter dated Feb. 1902).

There are a few other classes of which researchers into capital punishment should be aware: HO 324, consisting of registers and plans of prison burial grounds; 1834 to 1969, HO 291/92-117, which are files mainly dealing with murder; HO 347/8, which includes miscellaneous printed memoranda dealing with the issue of capital punishment; and T 207. The 'sheriffs' cravings' in this last class include claims for expenses from the Treasury in connection with taking custody of persons awaiting trial and the convicted awaiting execution for, although the organization of an execution was traditionally the responsibility of the high sheriff in any given county, the bulk of the costs involved were expected to fall on central, not local, finances.

6.1.3 Abolition of the Death Penalty

The first legislative attempt to abolish the death penalty as a punishment was made in 1867, but failed, as did further attempts in the 1870s, due to low levels of support in the House of Commons. This initial move for abolition was a reflection of the frustration felt by supporters at the failings of a Royal Commission on Capital Punishment which had been appointed in 1864. This Commission could not come to agreement on the fundamental question of whether capital punishment should be retained or abolished but did agree that the existing murder laws needed revision. They suggested a system of degrees of murder, so that the death penalty would be confined to the most horrible instances of premeditated homicide and murders committed in connection with other serious crimes against property or the person.

An attempt was made to enshrine the Commission's suggestions in legislation which failed, as did other bills on the same lines in the following decade. Just about the only substantive change to come about as a result of the Commission's deliberations was the nationwide move to private executions from 1868.

A more recent consideration of the death penalty was undertaken by the Royal Commission on Capital Punishment which was appointed by the home secretary in May 1949, under the chairmanship of Sir Ernest Gowers, to consider modifications to the law under which murder brought the death sentence, though not to consider whether it should be retained or abolished. The Royal Commission reported in September 1953 and, like its earlier counterpart, its conclusions resulted in no legislative changes. Minutes and evidence of the Royal Commission can be found in HO 301. A small number of related files can be found in PCOM 9. For example, PCOM 9/1374 records the views of the Prison Officers' Association, prison governors, chaplains, and medical officers, as expressed in evidence to the Royal Commission.

Capital punishment for murder was abolished in 1965 by the Murder (Abolition of Death Penalty) Act (13 & 14 Elizabeth II, c 71), but remains available for certain offences against military discipline, some forms of piracy and for treason.

6.2 Custodial Punishments

6.2.1 Transportation and the Hulks

The idea of transporting convicted criminals and social undesirables has a long history in Britain. An act of 1597-1598 (39 Elizabeth I, c 4) granted justices the power to send vagabonds abroad, though it is doubtful whether this was ever actually used. Between 1615 and 1661 some felons agreed to be sent to Virginia in exchange for a pardon through what was essentially an informal arrangement aimed at developing the colony. Statutes of 1661, 1666 and 1670 provided for the transportation of certain arsonists and thieves, but applicable offences were limited in range and the potential number of transportees was small. An act of 1717 (4 George I, c 11) greatly extended the scope of transportation by providing it as an alternative punishment to the branding or whipping of felons entitled to benefit of clergy.

By the 1770s, some concern was beginning to be expressed about the efficacy of this punishment which, to some, seemed not to be a punishment at all, but rather the chance of a fresh beginning at the expense of the state. Others argued that transportation provided cheap labour for the colonies whilst reforming convicts into the bargain. However, the discussion was soon shown to be fairly academic, as the American War of Independence intervened to deprive the British government of the only feasible overseas outlet for its convicts. Transportation was halted for a decade.

This cessation did not spur the politicians of the day to find an alternative. Rather, transportation remained central to the government's penal philosophy even after the loss of America, as shown by the Transportation Act 1784, which again promoted the exile of felons despite the fact that there was nowhere they could be sent. It was not until 1787 that the first fleet of convict ships left for Botany Bay in Australia, carrying 550 men and 191 women.[4] All future transportees would be sent to Australia or, after 1803, Van Diemen's Land (later Tasmania).

The Select Committee on Transportation (also known as the Molesworth Committee), which reported in 1838, recommended the abolition of transportation as a punishment (Sessional Papers, House of Commons, 669, 1837-8, XXII, I). At the same time, the Australian colonies were pressing for an end to transportation.

Terms of transportation of less than fourteen years were abolished by the Penal Servitude Act, 1853. The distinction between sentences of penal servitude and transportation was abolished in 1857, in effect abolishing transportation as a judicial sentence, though the home secretary continued to have the power to order transportation in specific cases until 1867.

It has been estimated that between thirty thousand and fifty thousand persons were transported to America before 1776 and a total of 163,000 persons to Australia and Tasmania in the following years. In the peak period of 1830 to 1839, the average number of convicts leaving for Australia was 4,100 each year.[5]

---

[4] Radzinowicz and Hood, p 467.
[5] Radzinowicz and Hood, p 468

The main Public Record Office classes dealing with transportation are:

- HO 7, including minutes of a House of Commons Committee on Transportation to West Africa as HO 7/1, and returns of convict deaths in New South Wales;
- HO 10, Settlers and Convicts in New South Wales and Tasmania, 1787-1859, which includes an 1828 census of settlers and ex-convicts in the colonies;
- HO 11, Convict Transportation Registers, 1787-1870, which are heavily used and therefore available on microfilm only; and MT 32, Surgeon Superintendents' Journals of Convict Ships, 1858-1867, including rules and regulations, list of convicts, medical reports and details of diet; HO 6/1-25, Judges' and Recorders' returns, 1816-1840, of convicts appealing for mercy, letters from prison governors, etc;
- HO 47/1-75, Judges' Reports on Criminals, 1794-1830; and
- PC 1/67-92, Correspondence relating to Transported Convicts, 1819-1844.

In addition, HO 347/4 includes some miscellaneous memoranda relating to transportation and prisons, and there are some contracts for the transportation of convicts, 1842-1867, giving the names of those concerned in TS 18.

Part of HO 20/13 is an extraordinarily detailed and lively record of a ship, the *Mandarin*, taking a cargo of convicted boys from Parkhurst Prison, together with a few ordinary passengers, from England to Australia in 1843. Written by the boys' superintendent, possibly a Mr Innes, it begins in optimistic vein as an almost daily account of the preparations and voyage, with numerous comments on the pleasing good behaviour of the boys. Later in the journal, problems are revealed including disagreements between members of the crew, and between the crew and the ordinary passengers; terrible and inexcusable drunkenness in almost everyone on board; inedible food offered in short measures; and an open hostility by the passengers towards the Parkhurst boys. This latter development, as Mr Innes suspected, was probably due to the fact that the passengers did not find out that the ship was carrying convicted criminals until it had set sail! In his entry for 1 September, Mr Innes described a fairly typical set of events, including the following, slightly bitter, comment.

I am almost tired [he wrote] of noticing the disgusting
conduct of passengers exhibited in communication with the
boys. One of the superintendents on duty [a trusted elder
boy appointed by Innes] came to me this morning to report
a conversation between himself and Mr Steadman which took
place last night in which the latter was evidently endeavouring
to provoke the boy, Day, who is nearly Steadman's equal in
size - to strike him by standing upon his toes, calling him a
d—d convict & then in anger a h— of h—. This same
"gentleman" the night after the Surgeon was assaulted by
the Captain, endeavoured to provoke him to assault, & was
about to strike him when prevented by another passenger.

This colourful account of life on board a ship carrying convicts, particularly
juveniles, is a rarity and could form the central text for a rewarding piece
of research.

6.2.2 Prison hulks

Even during the years when Britain had nowhere overseas to send convicts,
sentences of transportation, for seven or fourteen years or life, continued
to be awarded by courts of law. As a temporary expedient, the government
ordered that transportees were to be held on old ships, or hulks, moored
near naval dockyards, until transportation could resume. The first were
established in 1776 at Woolwich, with later hulks moored at Chatham,
Sheerness, Portsmouth and Plymouth.

After 1787, when transportation resumed, hulks continued to be used to
hold those waiting to be sent abroad. Indeed, such was the mis-match
between the availability of places for convicts on transport ships and the
number of felons being awarded sentences of transportation, that some
convicts served their whole sentence aboard a hulk. To spend a long period
on these vessels was probably a fairly unpleasant experience for all but the
most hardened. The hulks had a poor reputation among social reformers,
who emphasized the debilitating effects they had upon both the moral and
physical well-being of the prisoners within them. Discipline was almost
impossible to enforce in the cramped and squalid conditions: inmates were
said to improve their criminal knowledge, and sexual immorality and disease
were endemic.

Though the hulks were gradually replaced by purpose-built land prisons, this temporary expedient proved to be anything but short-lived. The last hulk in England was decommissioned in 1857; others continued to house British convicts in Gibraltar and Bermuda, where cheap labour was in great demand, till 1875. Towards the end of the eighteenth century, almost three-quarters of all convicted felons were held on hulks. This had fallen to a third by 1847, as a result of the introduction of land-based penitentiaries.

Records likely to be of interest to family historians are PCOM 2/131-137, registers of the hulks *Defence, Stirling Castle, Retribution, York* and *Europa* (at Gibraltar), for the period 1837 to 1860. Records of the *Cumberland* for the 1830s appear in ADM 6/418 and ADM 6/419; while the *Dolphin* has surviving records in ADM 6/420-423. A register of convicts aboard the prison ships *Antelope, Coromandel, Dromedary* and *Weymouth* at Bermuda between 1823 and 1828 is preserved as HO 7/3. HO 8 consists of 207 volumes of quarterly returns of prisoners both in hulks and land prisons, 1824-1876, which includes personal details, for example, behaviour. Those wishing to use this latter class will benefit from a detailed class list prepared by the Middlesex Family History Society and available at Kew. PCOM 5/1 consists of 'old captions' (i.e. copies of court orders for the imprisonment or transportation of convicts) and transfer papers, 1847-1857, relating to the inmates of hulks.

The Home Office generated convict prison hulk registers and letter books, dating from 1802 to 1849, which form HO 9 are extremely heavily used by visitors to the PRO and are made available only on microfilm at Kew. Class HO 7 includes some reports on conditions in the hulks and colonies. Researchers may also wish to use T 1 (with an index in T 2) which includes lists of convicts on hulks; the quarterly returns, 1802 to 1818, for prison hulks in T 38; and AO 3/292-296, accounts of convict hulks for 1830 to 1837.

6.2.3   Prisons and Penal Servitude

A great deal of research work over the past twenty-five years has focused on the nineteenth- and twentieth-century prison system. In the space available here, little more than a summary of the most important dates and organizations at work in the system and an indication of the richness of the surviving records of the prison system can be given. Readers whose concerns lie principally in this area would be well-advised to dip into some of the existing extensive literature in order to have a clearer understanding of the context in which prison records were created and where research could be most fruitfully undertaken. Newcomers to the subject will find Christopher Harding, Bill Hines, Richard Ireland & Philip Rawlings, *Imprisonment in England and Wales: A Concise History* (Croom Helm, 1985) extremely useful.

The history of imprisonment is briefly as follows. An act of 1609 established houses of correction, which were to be a feature of urban life till the nineteenth century. These were not prisons for felons, but were designed to hold vagrants and act as a deterrent to vagrancy. Justices of the Peace were instructed to appoint the staff of the houses of correction and to oversee their daily management. Separate places of detention also existed for debtors (described above in Chapter 3).

The Gaol Act 1823 required JPs to be responsible for the establishment and upkeep of county gaols, for the short-term holding of prisoners, which would be combined with houses of correction. As a result of the involvement of JPs in the county gaols and houses of correction, a researcher is likely to find much useful information amongst the records of the quarter sessions, which are held by local record offices.

The Gaol Act 1835 permitted the home secretary to appoint officers to staff convict prisons and also inspectors of county gaols. Some inspectors' reports for 1837 are in HO 20/4. In 1846, the Surveyor General of Prisons was appointed. In 1849 five inspectors of prisons were appointed. Prior to 1877, the majority of penal establishments were locally owned and run, with responsibility for convict prisons falling to the home secretary through the Directors of Convict Prisons, first appointed in 1850.

In 1877 the Prison Commission was appointed and under the Prisons Act of that year the local county gaols were transferred to government management. The Prison Commission was responsible for the maintenance of all prisons, the appointment of subordinate prison staff, the inspection of buildings and the conditions of prisoners. It submitted an annual report on each prison to the Home Office. Expenditure on prison matters, as authorized by the Treasury, between 1849 and 1934 can be traced in PCOM 13.

On 1 April 1963 the responsibility for penal establishments vested in the

Prison Commission was transferred to the home secretary. A Prisons Board was created as the principal executive body of the Home Office Prison Department and was similar in many respects to its predecessor, the Prison Commission. In recent years, this Board has been transformed into a semi-autonomous executive agency of the Home Office. Minutes of both the Prison Commissioners' and the Prisons Boards' meetings are available in PCOM 14. Records of the Prison Service agency will no doubt become available in due course.

The general series of the Prison Commission's registered papers is in two classes. Class PCOM 7, consisting of papers from 1838 to 1938 (though few papers are from before 1877) is divided into four sections:

a) *'General administration'* consists of files on accommodation, land, contracts for supplies, furniture and so on, together with a small but notable quantity of information on the Lady Visitors' Association established in 1901 with Adeline, Duchess of Bedford in the chair (PCOM 7/173-176). PCOM 7/174 includes a list identifying the lady prison visitors known to be working independently prior to the creation of the Association and also papers indicating that the ladies were to be discouraged from befriending suffragette prisoners;

b) *'Prisoners (general)'* covers files on mark systems for the promotion of good behaviour, uniform, diet, employment and corporal punishment;

c) *'Prisoners (special cases)'* category, which largely concerns the treatment of juvenile and young adult offenders; and

d) *'Staff'*, files on a wide range of personnel-related issues.

This general series of registered papers continues in PCOM 9 following much the same format, though it is somewhat easier to use as the class list has an index. Again, PCOM 9 has papers on just about every aspect of the prison system, from discussions of the nature of penal servitude to diet to prison disturbances. Further papers on prison disturbances will be found in HO 278, consisting of the papers of a 1960s inquiry into prison escapes and security chaired by the Earl Mountbatten; the papers and report in HO 318 of the Committee on the Prison Disciplinary System which was established in 1984; and HO 370, the transcripts of public hearings and seminars which took place as part of the Woolf Inquiry into Prison Disturbances at Strangeways and elsewhere in 1990.

The Penal Servitude Act 1853 introduced a system of extended imprisonment, known as **penal servitude**, as a substitute for transportation. Penal servitude was a different punishment from simple imprisonment. Those undergoing it were convicts, enduring a longer sentence, usually five years or more, with hard labour and in more austere surroundings than ordinary prisoners. Records at the PRO include information both on the convict prisons where sentences of penal servitude were served and on the local prisons where inmates were experiencing simple imprisonment.

Of all the many penal institutions established in the nineteenth century, **Pentonville Prison** is worth singling out, as it was built as a model prison for the operation of the **separate system**. This was a method of prisoner control and, it was hoped, rehabilitation which was intended to eliminate the bad influences which prisoners traditionally experienced in prisons through their association with other inmates. Human contact was to be limited to approved visitors, such as religious ministers, and the prison staff. There is some material on the building and upkeep of Pentonville, 1839-1885, in WORK 6/131. HO 20/13, contains a printed set of Rules for the Government of Pentonville Prison, 1842. An entry book for 1847-1849 forms HO 21/4. Other Pentonville records are mentioned below.

Family historians seeking an imprisoned ancestor and other historians looking for material for statistical analysis might benefit from the registers of prisoners, in PCOM 2, for the penal institutions of Bedford, Birmingham, Chatham, Dorchester, Millbank, Newgate, Parkhurst, Pentonville, Portland, Portsmouth, Shorncliffe, Wandsworth, Woking, Wormwood Scrubs, and Gibraltar. This class includes other prison records such as governors' reports, chaplains' journals, visitors' books, photographs (see fig.1) and registers of deaths which can add much to an understanding of prison life in the period. Other registers, for the 1840s to 1860s, for the local county prisons at Aylesbury, Bath, Leeds, Leicester, Northampton, Nottingham, Preston, Reading, Somerset and Wakefield are in HO 23, while yet further registers and returns of prisoners can be found in HO 24, including HO 24/12-14 for the female inmates at Millbank, 1843-1874. Quarterly returns of prisoners, 1824-1876, are preserved in HO 8. Printed lists of defendants held at Newgate, with the results of their trials for 1782 to 1853, form HO 77.

The Penal Servitude Act 1853 also introduced the **ticket-of-leave**, a licensing system under which convicts were released from prison and then, so it was planned, kept under supervision by the police or other accredited authorities. In fact, convicts released under this scheme often rapidly disappeared from sight. Licences to convicts to be at large under the provisions of the Penal Servitude Act 1853 are entered in PCOM 3 (men, 1853-1887) and PCOM 4 (women, 1853-1887), which are arranged in licence number order. PCOM 6 includes registers relating to PCOM 3 and PCOM 4, also arranged by licence number but with a serviceable index. There are some gaps. A later Home Office class, HO 169, consists of entry books of out-letters 1899-1906, concerning prisoners released on licence and the revocation of licences.

The release of prisoners under the parole system began in April 1968, under the provisions of the Criminal Justice Act 1967. The Parole Board was responsible for granting conditional early release from custody to suitable prisoners, subject to recall for misconduct. Annual reports of the Parole Board, 1968-1975, are to be found in BV 1.

A great deal of information on **prison staff** generally can be gleaned from PCOM 7 in which there are papers on issues as diverse as uniform, staff associations, pay and housing. However, papers on individual prison officers are somewhat sparse, and for the earlier period quarter sessions records may be more useful. Home Office out-letters relating to the appointment of prison staff can be found in HO 160 and HO 45: for example, HO 45/9558/71134B discussing the personal qualities thought appropriate in prison matrons; and HO 45/9717/A51528B on the salaries paid to subordinate officers in Broadmoor as well as local and convict prisons. Papers on labour disputes involving prison officers appear in the PCOM 7 class and also in HO 263 which contains minutes and evidence of a special committee, chaired by Mr Justice May, appointed by the home secretary in 1978 to examine the organization and management of the prison service in the UK, including prison officers' working arrangements and conditions of service, following a bout of industrial action. Evidence was received from a range of organizations such as the Civil and Public Servants Association (HO 263/24), the Howard League for Penal Reform (HO 263/31) and the Prison Psychological Service (HO 263/48); and there are also transcripts of oral evidence given by such well-known figures as Lord Longford (HO 263/195) The records in this class are closed at present, with some subject to extended closure of seventy-five years.

Other Home Office classes not yet mentioned but of importance to the subject of prisons are HO 22 which are general entry books of out-letters and papers for 1849 to 1921; the general printed circulars and memoranda from 1933 onwards which are held as HO 323; and HO 12, which includes original letters, memoranda and other papers on criminal matters dating from the mid-nineteenth century. This last class follows on from the Convict Establishment Papers for 1819-1844 among the unbound papers in PC 1. HO 45 and HO 144 should, as always, be carefully considered.

Finally, researchers should be aware that papers on prisons and the prison regime turn up throughout the modern public records. For example, reports on the education offered in prisons will be found in ED 196: ED 196/56 includes reports for the academic year 1953-1954 on the education offered to inmates of Wandsworth, Pentonville, Oxford and Brixton Prisons. Among Treasury records, you will also find examples of prison-related files: for example, the papers in T 221/77 discuss rewards offered in the inter-war period for information resulting in the prevention of prison escapes.

6.3   Non-Custodial Punishments

6.3.1   Fines

By the early nineteenth century, the laws governing fines were numerous and, in some cases, severe. A great problem with fines was that their effects were very uneven, so that what was an inconsequential sum for a rich person would be crippling for a poor one. Until 1879, JPs had no powers to permit the payment of fines in instalments and so, as a result, each year a large number of poor people were imprisoned for defaulting on a fine. Yet even the facility to pay by instalment did not eliminate imprisonment for non-payment. In 1904 about twenty per cent of those given fines were still gaoled for defaulting.[6]   As shown by the recent history of the Criminal Justice Act 1991, and the experiment of unit fines which linked the amounts of fines to levels of income, the fundamental difficulties underlying systems of financial penalties are far from being resolved.

Records relating to financial penalties are scattered through the public records and researchers will need to be persistent and careful in their

---

[6]. Radzinowicz and Hood, p 649

schools and summary jurisdiction, which were designed to divert juvenile offenders from the main criminal justice system and existing prisons which were held to be contaminating and stigmatizing of young and petty offenders.

There were a number of informal experiments by individual magistrates early in the nineteenth century which aimed at reducing the number of first-time and juvenile offenders subjected to the full possibilities of prescribed punishments. For example, in the 1840s the Recorder of Birmingham, Matthew Davenport Hill, attempted to find 'guardians' for young offenders who would be willing to take responsibility for their good behaviour. These were often the offenders' employers. While Hill had no legal sanctions which could be directed against 'probationers' who betrayed their trust, he would deal very severely with any such person brought before him for judgment a second time.

Another informal supervisory scheme was established by the Church of England Temperance Society, which employed missionaries in police courts from 1875 onwards. There was little evidence of official interest in diverting offenders from custody until the passing of the Summary Jurisdiction Act 1879, which allowed for persons convicted of a trivial offence to be discharged conditionally without punishment on giving security to appear for sentence if called upon. This built upon the ancient common law practice of using recognizances - an undertaking by a person before a court to appear again when called upon and to observe conditions imposed by the court, with or without providing sureties to it.

The probation system as established in 1907 owed a great deal to a scheme run in the State of Massachusetts. This had begun informally in c. 1841 when a cobbler from Boston, John Augustus, had begun to stand bail for offenders, having agreed to supervize and report upon them when called upon to do so. Augustus chose offenders with care and was helped in his work by the knowledge that since sentence was only suspended, should the offenders prove unco-operative they would still be subject to sanction. Augustus died in 1859, but his work was continued by volunteers until the introduction of a state-funded scheme for supervizing probationers in 1869.

In Britain, increasing dissatisfaction both with reformatories and the results of adult prisons led to a search for alternatives. As home secretary from 1880-1885, Sir William Vernon Harcourt instituted a wide-ranging project to gather both the opinions of judges and magistrates at home and more specific information on diversionary schemes abroad. The Howard Association, a charity formed to press the government for improvements in prisons and changes to penal policies, was instrumental in drawing the Massachusetts experiment to the attention of the Liberal government, though there were no immediate changes arising from Harcourt's enquiries.

The Probation of First Offenders Bill, introduced in the House of Commons in 1886 by Colonel C E Howard Vincent, was the first piece of proposed legislation to deal specifically with the idea of probation. Arguing that the dismissal of first offenders under the Summary Jurisdiction Acts was an unsatisfactory remedy of what was clearly a problem, he suggested that they should be subjected to police supervision under the Prevention of Crime Acts 1871 and 1879 for a period not exceeding the longest term of imprisonment to which they could have been sentenced. In effect, Vincent was suggesting that a ticket-of-leave scheme should be extended to all petty first offenders. This had a mixed reception from police and judicial authorities, with opposition from the Metropolitan Police and various members of the judiciary, but agreement from the chief constables of a number of provincial police forces, including Birmingham and Manchester. Under the weight of other political issues, the Bill was allowed to die, but the question of probation did not disappear.

Vincent and his allies in both Houses and in the country continued to apply pressure to the government, introducing a further Bill in 1887. The then home secretary, Henry Matthews, opposed the extension of police supervision to all first offenders under the Prevention of Crimes Acts and resisted the Bill until various changes were incorporated which largely undermined the whole purpose of the legislation and added little to the powers already available to courts under the Summary Jurisdiction Acts. A report of the Prison Commissioners in 1892 indicated that the provisions of the Probation of First Offenders Act 1887 were hardly ever used by the courts, sometimes, it seems, because magistrates had never become aware of the act's existence. Given that it added little to existing powers, the Act was largely an irrelevance.

Debate on the issue of probation continued to focus on juvenile offenders and the inadequacies of the reformatory school system. Supporters recycled the arguments which had been put forward in favour of the reformatory school almost half a century earlier: probation would prevent contamination of the lesser offender by the worse and would be cheaper for society both in the short and long term as it emptied institutions and prevented reoffending. Some pointed again to American models and Sir Evelyn Ruggles-Brise, chairman of the Prison Commissioners, added weight to their suggestions by showing that he was impressed with the probation systems he had encountered in a visit the the USA in the late 1890s. Sir Evelyn favoured the appointment of special probation officers, probably as part of the police authorities, with the sole task of supervizing offenders. Calls for the appointment of probation officers came from other quarters too, particularly from those also calling for special courts for the trying of juveniles.

Colonel Vincent had, by 1905, become convinced that the creation of both probation and children's courts were inevitably linked and, in that year, introduced a Bill which would allow magistrates to exclude the public from trials of persons under the age of sixteen. He abandoned this Bill in favour of a more comprehensive measure introduced by a Mr Tennant. Tennant's Bill fell due to lack of time. It was reintroduced in 1906 when it was not accorded a second reading.

Fortunately for the supporters of probation, the new home secretary was Herbert Gladstone, the son of William and a supporter of the principle of reformation and rehabilitation. He needed little encouragement to become involved in the creation of a piece of government-sponsored legislation introducing a system of probation which could potentially affect the treatment of all offenders. The Probation of Offenders (No 2) Bill was introduced to the Commons in March 1907. Couched in fairly general terms, among other provisions it allowed for the appointment of paid, full-time probation officers and outlined their principal duties. The Bill was discussed in both the Houses as a largely uncontroversial measure and received the Royal Assent on 21 August 1907. It came into force on 1 January 1908.

The first two approved probation officers were Miss A Iviny and Miss E Croker-King who were suggested to the Home Office by the renowned anti-suffragist and novelist, Mrs Humphrey Ward.[8] On the invitation of the home secretary, other organizations which had been involved in voluntary work among prisoners, such as the Reformatory and Refuge Union and the Salvation Army, provided additional candidates soon after.

---

[8] See HO 330/71, notes on the early history of the probation service, 1957

There are relatively few papers concerned with probation and the after-care of discharged prisoners amongst the classes held at the PRO. The Probation Series files for 1938 to 1972, forming HO 330, are the most immediately relevant. Created by the Probation Division of the Home Office, later the Criminal and Probation Department, then the Probation and After-Care Department, these consist of papers on a wide range of issues including general policy, legislation, the inspection of probation hostels (HO 330/5), complaints against probation officers, the funding of voluntary associations, and the probation inspectorate (HO 330/69). Minutes, 1950-1964, of the Probation Advisory and Training Board are held in HO 330/41-45.

HO 330/16-24 are important files of papers generated by the Departmental Committee to Inquire into the Probation Service, otherwise known as the Morison Committee, appointed in 1959 by the home secretary, R A Butler. Within the remit of the Morison Committee was the consideration of all aspects of the appointment of probation officers, their pay and conditions of service. As a result, the files give a very full picture both of the state of the probation service in the late 1950s and the fairly high regard in which it was held by those who came into contact with it from the official side of legal proceedings.

Other temporary bodies also considered the role of the probation officer. The Royal Commission on Marriage and Divorce, which was appointed in 1951, recommended (see HO 330/13) that the widely recognized and praised work of probation officers in offering a conciliation service following marital breakdown should be added to by giving them responsibility for supervision of children's welfare in divorce cases. The Home Office had no objection to this suggestion, but felt that it was a matter for the courts and the Lord Chancellor's Department to decide.

The central registered files of the Home Office, in HO 45, should also be consulted. Many of the pieces relating to probation deal with the provincial committees which controlled the locally-based organization of the probation service. A good example is HO 45/13386, which includes claims from local committees for expenses, their suggestions for changes to the rules governing probation, information on salaries and allowances, and correspondence clarifying the interpretation of the rules.

Records created by the **Central Aftercare Association (CACA)** and its predecessor bodies can be found in HO 247. The CACA was first established in 1901 as a charity called the London Prison Visitors' Association, changing its name in 1904 to the Borstal Association to reflect its new focus on young offenders discharged from Borstals. Its members were involved in finding work and accommodation for these discharged prisoners and, from 1908, implementing a statutory system of supervision. These activities are noted in the Association's printed annual reports which are open to researchers. Other files in this class, which deal with individual cases, are subject to a seventy-five year closure period. PCOM 9, Prison Commission Registered Papers Series II, 1901-1973, also includes papers relating to the CACA, PCOM 9/2276-2281 containing minutes and papers of the Association's Council and Executive Committee, 1949-1964.

A small amount of additional material can be found in the records of the assizes, particularly classes ASSI 86 to ASSI 92, containing medical and probation reports, although these classes are at present closed for 75 years.

Useful background reading: Dorothy Bochel, *Probation and Aftercare: Its development in England and Wales* (Scottish Academic Press, Edinburgh, 1976).

Chapter 7: YOUNG OFFENDERS

7.1. Dealing with Destitute and Delinquent Children before 1854

In any period of history, we can find evidence of some young people who have found themselves in trouble with their elders and with the formal authorities in society because they have broken either the law or accepted social mores. For the greater part of English history, young offenders were dealt with in a manner which was almost indistinguishable from the treatment of adult offenders. The first systematic attempt to reform criminal behaviour in the young in a manner tailored to their needs began in England with the activities of the Marine Society, founded in 1756.[1] In 1788 the Philanthropic Society began its operations in and around London, founding a home which would later become the government-certified Red Hill Reformatory for Boys.[2] There are doubtless other, less well known, examples of local action, the records of which might be found at local authority record offices.

Government involvement in attempts to treat juvenile criminals as a group distinct from adult criminals began with the establishment of the *Euryalus*, a hulk for young male offenders awaiting transportation. Certain of the PRO classes discussed previously (6.2.1) may help readers to assess whether this is an accurate judgment.

The next significant development was the establishment of Parkhurst Prison on the Isle of Wight in 1835. This was the first permanent government penal institution for dealing with juveniles. By the terms of its statute, both boys and girls could be accepted there, but in fact only boys became inmates. Parkhurst held convicted boys until 1868 when it was transformed into a women's prison. The PRO holds a reasonably large number of files relating to different aspects of the prison in the PCOM and HO classes: for example, HO 24/15 which is a register or return of inmates at Parkhurst for the years 1838 to 1863. Again, see chapter 6 of this guide for further suggestions.

---

[1] The National Maritime Museum has a substantial holding of the Marine Society's records from 1756 (ref: MSY/A).

[2] Records of the Philanthropic Society are held by Surrey Record Office at Kingston-upon-Thames.

It was not until the Parliamentary Select Committee on Mendicity of 1815-1816 devised a new label for criminality and bad behaviour among the young, 'juvenile delinquency', that it became widely accepted that young trouble-makers formed a distinct group in the criminal, and wider, population. 'Juvenile delinquency' was used to cover a wide range of behaviour, from boys larking about in an unruly manner in the street, to young girls offering sexual favours for money, to theft, assault and worse. It is important to be aware that 'juvenile delinquency' was a phrase used to describe much behaviour which was not strictly against the law. This wide interpretation impacted particularly upon girls. There is little doubt that some of the behaviour which was labelled deviant and unacceptable when exhibited by nineteenth century working-class girls would be considered acceptable today.

The Select Committee was examining the problems of vagrancy and crime which had grown out of the economic depression following the Napoleonic wars and which seemed to threaten public order and general social and political stability. Economic recovery led to a lessening of concern about criminality in general. However, the concept of the juvenile delinquent remained current and ready to become the focus of discussion when a fresh economic depression in the 1840s, together with middle-class anxiety over Chartism and the effects of the new poor law, led to a renewed interest in the level of crime.

Philanthropists and politicians believed society was under threat from the disaffected and criminal groups within it and they urgently sought a way of protecting the interests of those who remained respectable. In 1834, the national judicial statistics, which gave summary information about the types of crime being committed by various kinds of people, were presented in a new way. For the first time, they seemed to provide solid evidence that 'juvenile delinquents' were at the heart of the nation's crime problem. By breaking down the total annual offences by age it could be shown that, while a tenth of the nation's population was aged fifteen to twenty years old, this group produced a quarter of known offenders.

Though it was unclear whether the proportion of juvenile offenders was actually rising and despite the fact that the offences of which 'juvenile delinquents' were convicted were, in most cases, extremely trivial, an impetus was created for the establishment of a system of institutions known as reformatory and industrial schools which were expected to reform young criminals and rescue neglected children from the temptations of crime. These institutions are discussed in the next section.

They were not, of course, created in a historical vacuum. The most famous immediate ancestors of reformatories and industrial schools were the **ragged schools**, which, from the early 1840s, tried to reach the poorest, most neglected working-class children with a view to civilizing them and educating them into an acceptance of their station in the social hierarchy. Readers looking for archives of ragged schools should turn first to their local record office. The surviving papers of the movement's umbrella body, the Ragged School Union, now form part of the Barnardo's collection held by Liverpool University Archives Unit. Researchers will find very little information on these precursors to reformatory and industrial schools in the PRO. The main reason for this is that the ragged school initiatives were private, voluntary ventures, funded locally through charity and largely undertaken without the involvement of governmental bodies, either local or central.

7.2. Reformatory and Industrial Schools

The establishment of Parkhurst Prison was a step towards the specialized treatment of juveniles, but it remained essentially a prison with few concessions being made to the needs of adolescents beyond permission for the playing of some harmless games. Some philanthropists, such as Mary Carpenter in Bristol and Matthew Davenport Hill in Birmingham, argued that early exposure to prison lessened the individual's fear of it, so that it became an ineffective deterrent. Moreover, the prison was held to leave a stigma on the child, labelling it a criminal whilst its character was still undergoing change, and thus preventing it from obtaining honest employment in future. There was a very serious problem that young offenders were likely to be recidivists and thus experience many very short prison sentences to no good effect.

It was also the case that the majority of child prisoners were not in Parkhurst and were compelled to associate with adult inmates, which reformatory campaigners argued led to the juvenile leaving prison with enhanced criminal skills and a broader spectrum of ideas for illegal acts than he or she would have had otherwise. One writer summed this up by calling prisons 'pest-houses of contamination and vice, of impurity and immorality.'[3] The campaigners for reformatories believed that a prison should never be considered the right place for a minor. No matter how humanely a prison

---

[3]   Rev. John Dufton, *The prison and the school: A letter to Lord John Russell* (1848), p 18

was managed, it could never have satisfied those who believed that love, guidance, and education in a familial setting was the only way permanently to restore juvenile delinquents to respectable society. Growing public concern over juvenile delinquency led Parliament to pass the Youthful Offenders Act 1854 and the Industrial Schools Act 1857. These were subsequently amended and consolidated, most notably in 1866. The substitute to prison which was formally brought into being by these pieces of legislation had two parts: the **reformatory school** for children aged under sixteen who had been convicted of a crime and who were still to serve two weeks or more in an adult prison before being removed to the school; and the **industrial school** for children aged under fourteen who were deemed to be in danger of slipping into crime through their destitution, bad associations or the neglect of their parents. It is important to note that children sent by magistrates to the latter type of institution were supposed to be without any criminal conviction against them.

Reformatory inmates were sentenced to serve between three and five years in the schools, while industrial school inmates served until they were sixteen years old. This meant many children were detained for more than ten years. Over the second half of the nineteenth century, several hundred schools were founded by individuals, voluntary organizations and religious bodies, and well over a hundred thousand children passed through the doors of these institutions.

A certain amount of reorganisation of the system followed the passage of the Children and Young Persons Act 1933, after which the phrase 'approved school' replaced 'reformatory' and 'industrial school'. These institutions should not be confused with Borstals, which were intended for convicted young adults. Borstals are discussed below.

It should be noted that, even after the creation of the reformatory school system, children continued to be given sentences of detention in adult prisons without there being any intention that they would pass on to a school. Details of juvenile inmates can be found among many of the records indicated in the section of this guide dealing with prisons (6.2.3).

The PRO also holds a small number of items specifically dealing with children in prison. One of these is a maintenance account book for juvenile offenders held at Stafford Prison between 1863 and 1878 which forms PCOM 2/403. Each entry gives the individual's name, offence, date of conviction and length of sentence, calculating the cost of their maintenance at a rate of four shillings a week.

There is a great deal of fascinating material at the PRO dealing both with internal organization of reformatory schools and the government's relationship with them. As with other areas of penal history, HO 45 and HO 144 are rich sources of information on reformatories - indeed, it is impossible to give more than a few examples of the abundance which awaits the careful researcher. There are, for instance, a number of detailed files dealing with the organization of the government inspector's office and the problems his staff had to face in carrying out their work, including poor office accommodation and hostile parents of inmates (for example, HO 45/9830/B9213). Inadequate record-keeping in schools in relation to incidents of corporal punishment is noted by Inspector William Inglis in HO 45/9613/A9566. The poor educational standards of reformatory and industrial schools are also revealed, for example in HO 144/349/B14343. There are also significant pieces concerning the emigration of industrial school inmates, such as HO 45/9838/B10399A, which includes a memorandum of 1891 from Home Secretary Matthews stating that, in future, the permission of parents must be sought before a child could be sent overseas.

Various miscellaneous records of individual institutions, dating from 1855 to 1965, are held in HO 349. Most are subject to extended closure periods. However, future researchers should have access to some fascinating material on a par with the Stockport Industrial School register for 1866-1907 which forms HO 349/1. The registers and log-books could be extremely useful both for those seeking their wayward ancestors and for historians needing raw data for the statistical analysis of reformatory populations. Other papers on individual schools can be found in HO 45 (for example, HO 45/9931/B26218 on Middlesex Girls' Industrial School and HO 45/9720/A51731 on Mount Vernon Green Reformatory in Liverpool) and HO 144 (for example, HO 144/216/A49171 on Surrey Girls' Reformatory).

Some of the reformatory and approved school records generated by the Home Office Children's Department were subsequently transferred to the Ministry of Health and now form MH classes. The most significant of these are to be found in MH 102, the class list for which includes an index of the industrial, approved, remand and voluntary homes mentioned in the records, and a subject index. Many of the files in MH 102 deal with individual schools (see fig.10). For example, MH 102/22 concerns the

Northamptonshire Reformatory for Boys at Tiffield. The managers wrote to the home secretary in 1903 to explain that they had mislaid their original certificate, dating from 1856, and required a replacement. This file contains some very useful correspondence between Inspectors Legge and Robertson and the school managers on issues such as finance, building alterations, inspections and the number of boys permitted in the school. It also includes a set of school rules as approved in 1870 and a manuscript copy of the report by Legge of his inspection of the school in 1902. This class also includes in MH 102/2067 papers concerning the appointment and report of the Committee of Inquiry to Review Punishments in Prisons, Borstals, Approved Schools and Remand Homes, 1948-1950.

For the early part of the twentieth century, the Home Office entry books dealing with children's matters in HO 167 have some useful material to offer. For example, HO 167/12 is a Reformatory and Industrial Schools Entry Book for 1913-1914 which contains a wide range of out-letters, including correspondence with school managers on the issue and withdrawal of certificates, inspections, staff pay and conditions and the emigration of inmates. This volume has an index which permits researchers to identify letters relating to particular schools.

For the post-Second World War period, the inspection reports for a large number of approved schools, remand and voluntary homes are preserved in BN 62. The class list contains an alphabetical index of the institutions covered. Some of the reports, particularly those following unusual events such as disturbances or complaints of cruelty, are subject to a seventy-five year closure period. Nevertheless, this class will be of great importance for any study of the schools in these years. Also subject to extended closure periods is HO 360 which consists of files on approved schools from 1948 onwards.

Records relating to an investigation into one of the more scandalous incidents in the history of institutions for juvenile delinquents, namely irregular punishments at Court Lees Approved School, are preserved in HO 350. The findings of this inquiry led to withdrawal of the school's certificate by the home secretary in 1968. The published report of the inquiry is available at the PRO on microfilm; however, all twenty-two pieces in HO 350 are closed for seventy-five years.

There are many other classes which might be of some interest to the researcher into the treatment of juvenile delinquency in the twentieth century. These include MH 109, a collection of circulars sent by the chief inspector from the 1950s onwards to establishments entrusted with care of children, which range from the pay and conditions of staff to the rules governing the employment of approved school children in casual occupations. Attention should also be drawn to BN 29, which includes annual statistical reports for 1961-1970 on approved schools, remand homes and attendance centres (BN 29/375-382); papers relating the the Children and Young Persons Bill, 1962 (BN 29/435-459); and details of academic research projects of the 1960s and 1970s on approved schools (BN 29/472-488). Treasury consideration of the remuneration of staff in approved schools following the Second World War is recorded in T 221/17. Researchers might also find material of interest in BN 61, which consists largely of inspections of local authority child-care arrangements; BN 28, which includes some representative case papers of post-Second World War inmates at Waldernheath Girls Appoved School; and HO 361, which includes papers on Barnardo's homes from 1948 onwards.

7.3. Borstal

The institutions which came to be known as Borstals were aimed at offenders aged sixteen to twenty-one and were created to fill the gap between reformatory treatment for juveniles and prison for adults. The experiment began at Bedford Prison in 1900, when eight young adult offenders were placed under a new regime which was designed to be part reformatory and part prison with a strong emphasis on practical and moral training. The name Borstal was derived from the second stage of the experiment, when a section of the Borstal Prison in Kent was set aside to receive male youths from London who had received sentences of six months or more.

The experiment became a recognized element in the British penal system by the passage of the Prevention of Crime Act 1908, which permitted quarter sessions to sentence youths to Borstal Institutions for between one and three years. The minimum sentence was increased to two years in 1914 by the Criminal Justice Administration Act, which also gave magistrates the power to send suitable candidates for Borstal to the quarter sessions for sentencing. The great majority of individuals sentenced to Borstal training were male and the comparatively few young women receiving this sentence were kept in a special section of Aylesbury Prison.

The Borstal regime was to be austere, with a concentration on hard physical quasi-military training combined with lectures on morally improving subjects and a basic elementary education. A few files in the Ministry of Education classes shed light on the education offered by Borstals. For example, ED 149/3 describes the educational activities available at Reading Borstal in 1955, while ED 196/38 reports on the standard of education offered at Feltham Borstal in 1951-1952.

Inmates were also supposed to be given training in a trade, to help them stay honest when released, but this was generally given at a very low and inadequate level. PCOM 7/553, which discusses instruction in trades at Borstals between 1909 and 1917, is just one of the numerous pieces touching on this subject. It should be said that Borstal was not without its critics. PCOM 7/542 contains some stinging criticism of the system by the press, judges, magistrates and others in the 1920s. Nevertheless, the Borstal continued in use till the early 1980s, when the institutional means employed to deal with young offenders was reviewed and reformed.

Perhaps the most useful class for investigating the Borstal system is PCOM 9 which provides a mass of information. There are numerous files on the Borstal institutions at Aylesbury, Barington, Camp Hill, Durham, Feltham, Hatfield, Hollesley Bay, Lowdham, Pollington, Portland, Portsmouth, Reading, Rochester, Swinfen Hall and Usk. The class also contains discussion of general issues: for example, PCOM 9/36 concerns diet for Borstal boys (1931); PCOM 9/76, types of punishment used in Borstals in 1933; PCOM 9/184, the issue of clothing to Borstal boys on discharge (1937); and PCOM 9/443, notes on the suitability of the Borstal system for girls written in 1944. There are also relevant files in HO 45.

Records of the Borstal Association, which was a body established to supervise those discharged from Borstals, are discussed in the section concerning probation (6.3.3).

7.4. Juveniles before the Courts

Until the mid-nineteenth century, children charged with criminal offences tended to be dealt with in much the same way as adults, with their cases heard in the same courts and earning largely the same punishment for conviction, though it seems that juveniles were very rarely executed. This similarity in treatment was despite some recognition by the legal system that children were not simply miniature adults.

By the early nineteenth century, the rule that a child aged under seven was to be presumed incapable of committing a crime was well established. Children aged between seven and fourteen were presumed to be innocent of the intention to behave criminally, but this presumption could be challenged by the presentation of evidence of knowledge of guilt. However, the presentation of such evidence seems to have been merely a formality in the majority of cases. Over fourteen, defendants were believed to have full understanding of the morality of their actions.

Simultaneous to and connected with the philanthropic campaign to divert young offenders from adult punishment by introducing reformatory schools, was a pressure to treat them differently in the courts. Attention was paid in the first instance to increasing the number of children whose cases could be dealt with **summarily** (i.e. before a magistrate, without the case being sent for a jury trial in a higher court). The first substantive attempt to bring change was the introduction of a Bill into the House of Commons by Sir John Eardley Wilmot in 1840. However, change was delayed by a general fear that the denial of a jury trial to children would be unconstitutional. A change in the law did come in 1847, when summary jurisdiction was extended to those aged under fourteen charged with theft. More comprehensive change was brought about by the Summary Jurisdiction Act 1879 which gave magistrates power to deal summarily with all children under twelve charged with indictable offences.

Towards the end of the nineteenth century, dissatisfaction with ordinary summary jurisdiction led a wide range of organizations working in the fields of criminal justice and child-saving, including the Howard League and the National Society for the Prevention of Cruelty to Children, to propose and support the creation of a system of special courts for dealing with juveniles. A few areas, such as Birmingham, responded to these kind of pressures by voluntarily setting up special local juvenile courts. However, their establishment only became mandatory following the Children Act 1908.

The juvenile courts created by the act were to be special sittings of magistrates, from which the public were to be excluded, and which were to take place at a different location or at a different time from normal sittings. The juvenile courts were given both criminal and civil jurisdiction and the power to deal with all defendants aged between seven and sixteen, with the exception of those accused of murder. Importantly, the Act protected the right of a child accused of a criminal offence to elect for trial by jury. The juvenile court system created by the 1908 act was largely unchanged until the Children and Young Persons Act 1969.

When researching juvenile courts, you should bear in mind that they are now referred to as **youth courts** and, since 1992, have dealt with offenders under the age of eighteen.

Generally, local record offices should be the first port of call for researchers trying to find out more about the experience of juveniles before courts of law. While the PRO holds some papers dealing with juvenile courts, they are fairly miscellanous and scattered. The HO, LCO and BN classes contain the greatest number. For example, HO 291/52 includes a draft report on juvenile courts in 1959 written for inclusion in the Eighth Report of the Home Office Children's Department.

The records of an official Working Party on the Planning of Juvenile Courts in 1953 are preserved in HO 330/71. These include a summary history of the work of the probation service in connection with juvenile justice and plans of model juvenile courts.

A file containing papers reviewing the work of the London County Council Children's Department in relation to juvenile courts (BN 29/85) contains a discussion of the proportion of cases resolved outside the home area of the accused juvenile. Some official papers and incidental correspondence dealing with the reorganization of the petty sessions and juvenile courts in the early 1960s is to be found in BN 29/421.

APPENDIX I

How to find the correct reference when using Home Office: Registered Papers (HO 45)

The records contained in class HO 45 are useful for almost all areas of the legal and criminal history of the nineteenth and twentieth centuries. Unfortunately, it is one of the most difficult classes to use as the process of finding a complete and correct reference to a particular piece is different for records of different periods. This arises from the history of record-keeping in the Home Office.

A Central Registry was established in June 1848. From then till 1871, letters and papers received at the Home Office were numbered consecutively on receipt, starting afresh at 1 January each year. Papers from the years 1841 to 1848 were numbered retrospectively. Between 1848 and 1852, a note of all papers received was entered in the registers which now form HO 46. Papers relating to criminal matters which were received between 1852 and 1871 are in HO 12, with registers now in HO 14.

Between 1871 and 1880, all incoming papers were registered in a series running from 1 to 100,000. In 1880, a new series of consecutive numbers was begun with an A prefix. In 1883, further sequences, with B and V prefixes were begun, followed in 1885 by a sequence with an X prefix. This sequence was continued until August 1902 when a new system was introduced, with files being registered in a six-figure series starting at 100,001. In 1949 this system was in turn replaced by separate series of files for each Home Office function or area of interest, each distinguished by letter symbols (for example, MNP series for Mental Patient files).

The remainder of this appendix is designed to assist you in ordering from the HO 45 class.

(i) HO 45 pieces pre-1871

When ordering a piece from HO 45 for the period before 1871, you need cite only the class number (HO 45) and the piece number which is given in the left hand column of the class list. For example, HO 45/7750 is the complete reference for a file on the flogging of juvenile offenders by the police.

HO 45	Date	Description
		JURIES
7316	1862	Jury lists: reception of lists to be by clerks of justices in special petty sessions instead of by high constables (Juries Act 1862) (L.O.O.54)
7533	1864	Juries in Criminal Cases Bill
7742	1865	Dentists: proposed exemption from jury service
7788	1865	Special juries: London and Middlesex; inconvenience and remedy suggested
7908	1866	Inspector of schools: inconvenience of jury service
8328	1870	Exemption of inhabitants of Westminster from serving on juries at any sessions outside city and liberty of Westminster: objected to by Middlesex magistrates but maintained by Juries Act 1870
8388	1871	Property tax commissioners: exemption from serving on juries annulled by Juries Act 1870
8392	1870	Grand jury's "True Bill" in a criminal case mislaid and not presented to court

Page of class list; page beginning Juries.

(ii) HO 45 pieces between 1871 and 1920

This is the most complex section of the class from which to order. You need to consult both the class list and a separate finding aid called the **packing list**, which refers to the boxes in which the files are kept.

You may, for example, be interested in the treatment of juveniles by the criminal justice system in the nineteenth century. One piece which might be of interest is HO 45/9670/A46404, a file of papers on the establishment of Manchester Mill Street Day Industrial School, 1887-1889. The reference to this file consists of HO, the lettercode; 45, the class number; and 9670/A46404 the piece number, representing the box in which the item is kept and the original file number. To find this complete reference, you need to go through the following stages:

(a) The class list for HO 45 is arranged by blocks of years and you will need to go to the correct binder covering the years which you are researching; in this case, 1879-1900.

(b) There is a list of subject headings at the front of the binder covering the various activities of the Home Office during the period in question. In this instance, you should select CHILDREN. Turn to the main part of the binder, which is arranged alphabetically by subject heading, till you find the beginning of the section entitled CHILDREN. By scanning this section, you will eventually find the entry for the piece containing papers relating to Manchester Mill Street Day Industrial School. This entry provides a brief title outlining the contents of the piece and their covering dates, together with the sub-number of the piece which is the original Home Office file number (in this case A46404). Where a sub-number of the piece has a letter at its beginning or end this must always be included in the complete reference used to order it.

(c) You now have two parts of the reference needed to order this file, i.e. HO 45/............./A46404. The only remaining stage is to complete the reference to the piece number.

(d) Turn to the binder marked **HO 45 Packing List Post 1871** which is shelved next to the HO 45 class list. This is arranged internally by grouping years: 1871-1878, 1879-1900, 1901-1909, 1910-1919, 1920, 1921-1922; with each year noted separately between 1923 and 1950. (There is no packing (or box) list for the period before 1871.) Open the packing (or box) list binder at the section with dates covering those of the piece in question (in this case 1879-1900).

CHILDREN - (Continued)

1886	Orders of discharge and transfers of inmates of Industrial and Reformatory Schools should bear signature of Secretary of State L.O.O. 811.	A43449
1886	Alterations in authorised numbers of a school to be endorsed on original certificate by Secretary of State.	A45132
1886-88	Scheme for emigrating children to Canada in lieu of committal to Industrial Schools.	A46505B
1886-89	Provision in Industrial Schools for children of Jewish religion.	A46642
1887	Scheme for division of existing Industrial Schools into separate schools for boys and girls. Transfers effected in some schools.	A46324
1887	Discharging of boys to enter Royal Navy to be conditional on acceptance by Naval Authorities.	A46480
1887-88	Prevention of Cruelty to Children Act, 1886.	B825
1887-89	Establishment of Manchester Mill Street Day Industrial School.	A46404
1887-93	Reformatory Schools Bill, 1892.	A46656

Reference HO 45	1879-1900 FILE NUMBERS				HO 45
9664	A43825; A44058; A44207; A44343; A44602;	A43947; A44128; A44208; A44391; A44607;	A43992; A44145; A44209; A44402; A44607B.	A44039; A44194; A44277; A44542;	A44051; A44206; A44280; A44585;
9665	A44656; A44720; A44909; A45094; A45356;	A44656B; A44765; A44968; A45095; A45358;	A44689; A44889; A45068; A45132; A45359.	A44690; A44898; A45080; A45144;	A44711; A44905; A45092; A45229; A45281;
9666	A45364; A45529; A45613; A45829; A46019; A46170;	A45376; A45532; A45656; A45846; A46048; A46182;	A45390; A45537; A45671; A45983; A46084; A46202;	A45417; A45552B; A45698; A45990; A46147; A46211.	A45480; A45562; A45767; A46018; A46163;
9667	A46213; A46379;	A46260; A46380;	A46295; A46630B;	A46308; A46382.	A46324;
9668	A46382B;	A46382D;	A46382I.		
9669	A46384; A46397E.	A46388;	A46397;	A46397B;	A46397C;
9670	A46397H; A46408;	A46397L; A46416(1-75);	A46400;	A46403; A46416(76-110).	A46404;
9671	A46416B; A46443.	A46425;	A46425B;	A46430;	A46438;

his margin t to be ed.

Detail from page of class list (above) and from the packing list showing file no A46404.

(e) Each page of the packing (or box) list up to 1923 is arranged in this way: piece number in the left hand column, with sub-numbers grouped together in the right hand portion of the page. The sub-numbers are arranged in ascending number order reading from left to right across the page. Look through them till you find the sub-number which you are wishing to order (in this case A46404). Then look across to the left hand column. Read off the piece (or box) number in this column (in this case 9670).

(f) You now have the full reference for this file, HO 45/9670/A46404, and can order it successfully. The PRO's document ordering system will reject any attempt to order this document which does not consist of the three parts to the reference.

(iii) HO 45 pieces post-1920

For later records, though the packing (or box) list exists, there is no need to consult it unless you only have a note of the reference and wish to locate the subject heading where it is to be found in the class list. For example, to order a particular file on immorality amongst young girls, 1934-1937, you need only quote HO 45/21072. The piece number is given in the left hand column of the class list. You do not need to cite the file number which also appears, in this case 677925.

SUMMARY - HO 45: Is Your Reference Correct?

Records before 1871 and after 1920:
Reference should consist of lettercode, class number and piece number, e.g. HO 45/19579.

Records between 1871 and 1920:
Reference should consist of lettercode, class number, piece number and sub-(file) number e.g. HO 45/9362/33918.

To order the latter document it should be requisitioned, *via* the computer, as follows:

Lettercode or Map prefix HO	Class no/ Sub-no 45	Piece number or Map number 9362/33918	To end (range)

		HO 45	

HO 45	Date	Description	File No.
		CHILDREN	
20872	1914-1933	Employment in hotels, theatres and other places of public entertainment: protests and investigations into long hours worked.	268093
21084	1935-1936	Public Health Bill and Act, 1936.	684187
21106	1936	Gold Coast proposal to withdraw right of appeal from offenders sentenced to be whipped: memorandum setting out objections.	694708
21072	1934-1937	Juvenile Courts: immorality amongst young girls.	677925
21107	1936-1937	Juvenile Court Panels: reactions to circular suggesting appointment of younger justices.	694989
21119	1937-1942	Juvenile Courts: composition; age of magistrates.	699375/1-71
21120	1942-1943	Ditto	699375/72-100
21055	1933-1939	Juvenile Courts: publication of names of juveniles in newspapers	661842/1-48

Illustration of class list showing page beginning piece 20872, Children: Employment in Hotels, file no.268093

INDEX